Storytelling *for* Pantsers

How to Write and Revise Your Novel Without an Outline

Storytelling *for* Pantsers

How to Write and Revise Your Novel Without an Outline

Annalisa Parent

LAUREL ELITE BOOKS

BUFFALO, WYOMING

Laurel Elite Books
412 N. Main St., STE 100
Buffalo, WY 82834
www.LaurelEliteBooks.com

Additional copies of this book may be purchased at: StorytellingForPantsers.com

Book layout and cover design by Faithe Thomas

Cover photo by Caitlyn Fleet, Model: Nate Williams

Storytelling for Pantsers/ Annalisa Parent. — 1st ed.
Softcover ISBN 978-1-947482-01-2
Hardcover ISBN: 978-1-947482-02-9
eBook ISBN: 978-1-947482-03-6

Library of Congress Control Number: 2017949249

Printed in the USA

Dedication

For Dad, who was one of my first teachers and who is still always there to answer whatever random questions I call to ask.

And for Ma – even if you always insisted we call you Mom – for teaching me the secret in the sauce in so many ways.

Introduction

What is a Pantser?

BRIEFLY PUT, A PANTSER is someone who writes by the seat of his pants (or briefs, if you're that kind of guy. Hey, no judgments here.).

He—or *she*—is the writer who, like Spock and Bones, goes "where no man has gone before": the unchartered territory of a novel without an outline.

Scary? Sure. An adventure? *Always.*

This book is intended to help those of us seat-flyers get at least *some* grounding in what we do, and to find and use a system in the chaos that is pantsing.

This book is for you if you:

 Have started a novel at least 68 times (the *same* novel) and only written the first chapter

𝚫 Write chapter one. And then chapter five. And then chapter two. Etc.

𝚫 Need to *write* to discover your story. (It's highly likely you're also the kind of writer who, when asked what writing is like, says, "I just watch my characters and write down what they do.")

𝚫 Get lost in the weeds of writing and revision because portions of your novel are in different phases of the writing process.

𝚫 Feel frustrated because "Dang it; writing's hard enough. Why do I always have to complicate it?"

𝚫 Think the cover of this book is cool, or wear pants. Because, hey, the cover *is* cool. So are you, and *so* is this book. (Who says you can't judge a book by its cover? Pshaw.)

So read on.

Contents

What is a Pantser? vii

Part I – Pantsing

ANALOGIES GALORE.. 1
Writing is like a...Printer?..2
Analogy Number Four (Three, Sir!) 3
Did I Say That Was The Last Analogy?..4

HOW DO I BECOME A PANTSER? 7

MA'S SAUCE 9
Fiction Vortex, what? 11
How to use this book 15

Part II – Mind & Gray Matter

OPTIMIZING YOUR BRAIN'S INNATE POWER 19
The Creative Zone 19
When is it time to invite the inner critic in for dinner?.........21
But wait, there's more. 25
Emotional Hijacking...26
Umm, Annalisa, this isn't a science book. 26
Braggy-brag moment..27

FINDING THE CONFIDENCE TO WRITE 29
Is My Writing Good Enough?..29
Why is it taking me so long to finish my manuscript? 29
I've been writing for so long. Haven't I gotten it right yet? ...30
What's the right way to write?...32
One is the loneliest number..33
There's a U in the middle of Truth 34
There's a monster under the bed...36
To err is human 39
Oh, Doubting Thomas...41
When to invite the inner critic in for dinner 47
Winning the Lottery..48
What if Nobody Likes me?...51

Big Important Strategy...52

FINDING THE TIME TO WRITE....................................55
   If books could whisper in your ear.....................................60

HOW TO FIND THE KIND OF SUPPORT YOU NEED TO
HELP YOU BE YOUR VERY BEST WRITER 65
   Feedback..65
   No pressure or anything 66
   Reader Feedback vs. Writing Feedback..............................70

QUALITIES OF WRONG FEEDBACK 73
   Wrong source 73
   DANGER: Ego Ahead 74
   Unqualified for the job 77
   Oh yes, darling, my manuscript is with my beta readers......80
   Poor timing..81

QUALITIES OF QUALITY FEEDBACK 83
   Quality feedback is based on how your brain works 83
   Feedback that moves the writing forward 85
   Expertise in the Publishing Industry.................................86
   More Analogies Ahead 88
   What happens when you find the right kind of feedback? ...89

Part III – Craft

What do agents complain about when they think no one's
listening? 93

CHARACTER AND CONFLICT WITH A LITTLE BIT
OF SETTING THROWN IN 97
   How pantsers get to know their characters 98
   Life is like an analogy..98
   The number one thing 102
   Your characters must be relatable.................................119
   Quirks...120
   A note about psychology 121
   How much detail should I include?.................................122
   Conflict... 124

Wait, weren't we going to talk about setting?......................128

Confused yet? 129

WHAT IS PLOT? 131

Plot-Driven vs. Character-Driven 132

What's Unique for Pantsers...135

Empathy Moment Brought to You by the
Letter K for Knitting..136

The Parts of the Story...137

WHAT IS PACING? 157

Are we there yet?..158

THE SECRET TO THE SAUCE 161

BALANCE 163

Stake and a side of fries 163

I Gots to Use It...164

Emotional Intensity 168

Make Up Your Mind!...173

AND...ACTION! 175

On Being a Character..178

The key to a good novel is to have every aspect in balance ..182

The Rainbow Bridge from Balance to Economy 182

ECONOMY...183

On Being a Character...187

The Rainbow Bridge from Balance to Economy 187

Being economical with your time 189

What Makes a Page Turner?..189

ENTER Professor Parent [STAGE RIGHT]....................190

Economy in the exposition 193

A note on formulas 204

Remember the Weaving?...205

Make it complicated. Don't make it complicated. 207

CLARITY..209

Chewing GUM lose its flavor? 209

You get what you pay for...211

Moving your novel from B- to A+ 212

Less is More.. 213

Cut the Melodrama 214

While we've got the ax out.............................. 215

Why is it tempting to include too much detail?........... 216

But what about grammar?................................ 217

Are you gratuitously thesaurusing?

STOP IT. NOW. I mean it. 220

Pesky Little Present Participle......................... 222

Why do you have a love triangle with verb tenses?....... 224

Over-excitement.. 225

Who's driving this car?.................................... 226

Who you dissing?.. 227

HOW TO PUBLISH 231

They've got their mindset in order.................... 234

Let's do the timewarp (again) 237

You don't need a class. You need a program. 242

Getting the Feedback loop right....................... 253

Invest in a Program that Works....................... 258

RESOURCES.. 265

WORKS CITED.. 269

FINAL COMMENTS 273

Acknowledgements 276

Love the Secret Sauce..................................... 277

About the Author 278

Part I

Pantsing

ANALOGIES GALORE

BEING A PANTSER IS like being an architect who builds a little bit of each floor from

bottom to top

and then

bottom to top again

rather than the way we do it in the real world: foundation, walls, roof, etc.

Now, of course this kind of construction wouldn't work in the real world of physics, but it *is*, nonetheless, how we pantsers create structure for our novels.

We build a wall floating in the air. Then we fill in a fireplace on the ground floor. Chimney! Kitchen chair...

It's no wonder we can't see a house in that muddle. For a long time, it's just a bunch of potential, a jumble of stuff, incohesive. It takes a lot of time and patience to connect what we've done and to start to see the house coming into form.

This book is intended to help you to start to see your patterns more quickly, and to learn strategies to embrace the process. (Because I am sorry to say: You're stuck with it.)

Writing is like a...Printer?

Remember those old dot matrix printers? They would spread a layer of dots, and then go back over and spread another. And then another. Is it a recipe? A photo of Grandma? Part of the fun as a kid was the mystery to see what would reveal itself at the end.

Like one of those old dot matrix printers, we have to layer upon layer until the final manuscript is done. It's hard to see what it will become in the third or fourth layer of dots. We've built something, but we don't know *what* yet.

Analogy Number Four (Three, Sir!)

My friend, the great writer Jill Schefielbein, has one of the best analogies I've heard for the writing process.

When you put together a puzzle, she asks, are you the one who builds the frame first, and then fills in the pieces? Or do you just dive in, start to look for color and pattern matches?

Now look, this is not a book about putting together puzzles. (Puzzling for Pantsers? Hmm. On second thought, 'tis silly.)

But I think she's onto something. (Of course she is; she's brilliant.)

Gratuitous photo of me and Jill so I am brilliant by association

As pantsers we just wander in, start to take in what's around us. Place pieces, look for other pieces that share similar themes, build slowly into a cohesive whole.

It's a beautiful process, but much like building a puzzle in this fashion, it has its frustrations.

That's the main problem for us pantsers—losing sight of the forest for the trees for the forest and for the trees again. Around and around we go. It's hard to know what the heck it is we're doing day in and day out.

Here's one last analogy, and hopefully this one will help you to see this success is not only possible but *how* it is possible.

Consider a sculptor. Now, I'm not a sculptor, but I can imagine his process. He's got a big block of granite, it's nothing really, just stone. He's got a concept and he starts to chisel away. The work looks like very little for a very long time. Chip chip chip. Still a Big Blob day, after day, after day. Yet he returns. Chip, chip, chip.

And eventually his vision starts to take form. The arm will be here, there a leg. Up until that point, all he had was a faith in his vision.

Did I Say That Was The Last Analogy?

Think of Michelangelo painting the Sistine Chapel or Monet painting the water lily murals one dot at a time. These artists were close to the canvas (ok, ok, ok, or the *ceiling*) without the wide view or option of stepping away to see the big picture.

Art has been created this way for centuries—with a vision, a rough plan, and raw talent. And yet so many advisers tell fiction writers to outline before they go. No, I don't disagree that a rough outline, a sketch, *can* help pantsers. Many painters sketched before painting—but they didn't draw a paint-by-numbers on the canvas for themselves.

Art is much more complicated than that. Rather, these artists sketched ahead of time: they drew to feel the curve of the apple or a cheek, to get a feel, a direction before plunging in—as you do with character sketches or plot diagrams.

Yes, by all means, *think* before engaging, but please, oh please, if you are a pantser: Do *not* attempt to apply too much structure. I know it's tempting, but pantsers who do so end up with books that feel formulaic or overworked.

Instead, give yourself the freedom to let writing be the art it is—an exploration—let it lead sometimes, but above all, be in *flow* with your work. That, my fellow pantsers, is where the magic happens.

Even writers who outline muddle through revision and what goes where. Their process has some differences, but by and large, they ask the same questions we do—just in a different way.

Nobody has it better off, I promise.

Also, I want to express here that I am not categorically opposed to outlines. To every thing a season, and a purpose...

HOW DO I BECOME A PANTSER?

You don't.

Sorry.

Here is what I believe: There are pantsers and there are out-liners. We are born not made. Additionally, there are projects that warrant pants-ing and there are projects that warrant outlines.

The most important thing is to find out the kind of writer you are, and be that writer!

Secret Sauce:
The most important thing is to find out the kind of writer you are, and be that writer!

(Look, that one piece of advice was so important, I used an exclamation point. Exclamation points are a no-no. Fitzgerald said so. I'll tell you more about that in the clarity section.)

If you are an outliner, it's highly unlikely you will transform into a pantser. And vice-versa.

Even odder, you may use a more detailed outline at times, and be a total and utter pantser other times.

When I write fiction, I am a First Class Pantser. When I write nonfiction, hand over the outline, baby.

It's a quirk. (I have many, trust me.) It's just the way my brain works.

Your lovely brain works the way your lovely brain works. Embrace it, and be wonderful you.

We'll talk more about your brain later.

MA'S SAUCE

Now that we understand a little bit about what pantsing is, let's look at how a pantser's process differs from an outliner's.

Before I continue, however, let me take a moment to say that this book (and any other you've read on writing craft) must, by the nature of book formatting, be organized in a linear fashion: chapter one, chapter two, and so on, right?

HOWEVER

Writing and revision is a cyclical process, especially for pantsers.

What do I mean?

Let's play a little game. Here's what you need:

- A piece of string 2 to 3 feet long
- A weight to tie to the end of it (a pen will do)
- Four index cards
- Something to write with (Hey, maybe that pen serves two purposes; look at that. We'll talk more about *that* later too.)

Place your cards on the floor about 2 feet from each other in the north, east, south, and west positions. Write on the cards, in any order you choose (one word per card): character, plot, pacing, clarity.

Ok, now stand with your string and pen so that the pen is positioned in the center of your cards. Start swinging it around in a circle so it moves around (clockwise or counterclockwise, whatever your pleasure). Get some good momentum going so your pen flies over each one of these ideas, then start lifting the string every so slightly. Continuing the circling motion, bring the pen up to your waist, your chest.

How high can you bring it?

(If you actually played this game, I'd love to see your photos @annalisaparent #FictionVortex.)

Fiction Vortex, what?

What we've demonstrated in this activity is the non-linear writing process for pantsers, and how the craft principles will be your touchstones over and over again through the process.

The raising of the string higher and higher is time passing, the evolution of your manuscript. As the string moves up and up and up, you will revisit the concepts of craft, and your thinking will advance.

Take character for example: The way you think about character when the pen is at your feet will be different from the way you think about it when you come around to character again when the pen is at your knees, which in turn will be different from how you think about this same concept when the pen is at your waist. The same evolution will happen for each of the craft elements as you move through the vortex and toward the completion of your novel.

Same concept, new point of view because your story has evolved, you've put in more pieces, built more of your house, printed more lines on your printer (whichever analogy works for you).

To further complicate the issue, *your* story writing vortex and *my* story writing vortex will need similar elements, but not in the same proportion or order. My characters are not your characters, the struggle of mine is not the struggle of yours—so our vortexes, our processes, have similar elements, but are not identical.

Thank goodness, as this is what leads to the richness of the fiction canon and the reason why there are still stories to tell.

However, this lack of step-by-step design is also what makes *writing* so complicated for pantsers—not impossible, but complicated.

Let's step into the kitchen for a moment.

I come from a large Italian family on my mother's side. I've told you enough already to know that spaghetti sauce is *sacred* in our house. Now, if you asked my mother for the Palumbo family spaghetti sauce recipe, well, she tell you to get lost (or to go to Naples, technically) because the sacred sauce is a Family Secret. (Family Food Secrets. Is that just an Italian thing?) But if she *did* tell you this secret in the sauce, good luck writing it down.

At the risk of being taken out and shot, here's how my mom makes sauce:

- Fresh tomatoes or canned fresh tomatoes from the garden. How much? About that much.
- Oregano. How much? Umm, a pinch, maybe a little more. Stir it and see.
- Garlic. How much? Well, a lot. (We are Italian, re-member?) A clove, another clove, then some more...

You get the picture. The same is true for all the ingredients. (You didn't think I was actually going to give you the recipe, did you? What, do I want to get disowned?)

This sauce simmers (and makes all of us drool) for a minimum of 24 hours and every hour or so, Ma gets up, stirs the pot thoroughly, takes a taste off the wooden spoon, adds a pinch of this, a shake of that, stirs again, replaces the lid, and moves on.

This thing we do—writing, being a pantser—is a lot like Ma's sauce.

I can write an entire chapter on oregano, its merits, why it's essential to sauce, the ratio of oregano to garlic, but what?

1. It's only one ingredient. You have to understand them *all* and *how they play together* before you're really ready to make a sauce.

2. You've got to keep going back and tasting, tweaking and revising. Add a little character, a pinch of pacing...

Now, I know I've made you hungry and you've already called Antonio's for a reservation tonight, but here's the bottom line: This idea is the most important one in this book:

You don't need a checklist or a recipe or a—*anything* else.

Ma knows the sauce is done when she tastes that it's done. The sculptor knows she's done when she *feels* it.

Give yourself permission to be an artist. Feel within your piece. Breathe with it and sense it.

It might sound a little out there, but the more you can have a sense for the *pulse* of your piece, in other words how all these elements are working together, the better your writing will become, and the easier.

Don't be afraid to go back and taste. I go back and reread what I've written as a regular part of the process, to get the flavor for where I've been, and where I want to go next.

Also, be *patient* with yourself. Ma was not born knowing how to make sauce—no matter what she tells you about her Italian blood.

There were times, I'm sure, where there was too much garlic, not enough oregano—over time and *through making sauce*, she learned when to add this, when to turn up the heat, etc.

Secret Sauce:
These pots tell you the secret sauce to writing throughout the book. Ah ha! Pass the Parmesan, please.

So, too, will you learn the nuances of writing through active practice. This is why *writing* is the most important thing you can do to become a writer.

How to use this book

Because of the vortex nature of the writing process and because there's no formula for writing a fiction book, I strongly suggest that you read through the book in its entirety once, and then go through a second and third time as you apply the elements to your current writing project.

Hey Smarty Pants.
Line your pockets with *this*.

You know you want to take notes. Well, we've got you covered. Download the free *Storytelling for Pantsers* notetaking outline at www.writing-gym.com/notes

One of the things you'll notice about this book is it follows the course of that vortex. So, we'll talk about characters, for example, in the section called "character." (Genius, that, no?) Then, because the string swings round and round again, we'll talk about how character evolves throughout your writing process.

We will continue to revisit craft and advance it to the next level.

Now before you turn the page, I want you to do one teensy little thing for me: Give up on the dream that you're just going to sit down and write a novel from beginning to end. That's not the way your brain works, and that's ok.

(Have I mentioned that you're a pantser?)

In my own process, once I got over the drive to work through a novel in a linear fashion or, more importantly, the belief that that's the way it was "supposed" to be done, I was able to be far more productive and the drafting process became a whole lot more fun.

Let's talk about your brain.

Part II

Mind & Gray Matter

OPTIMIZING YOUR BRAIN'S INNATE POWER

DO YOU EVEN KNOW where you are? Most writers do not because they don't know the connection between writing and the brain. Well, you're in luck for having chosen this book. I'm about to show you the secret world of your brain.

The writing process is broken into two distinct phases, and one of the biggest mistakes even experienced writers make is confusing the two. Look, I don't make this stuff up: It's neuroscience. As pantsers it is of especial importance to honor the way the brain works.

The Creative Zone

Creativity is like play. When you were a child making up games or narratives for your figurines to act out, you didn't stop yourself or say, "Oh no, Fun Loving Malibu Barbie would never do *that.*" Right? You just went with the flow, hunting imaginary dragons, fighting imaginary cowboys without questioning: "Will this work?" "Does that make sense?" "Am I getting enough symbolism in here?"

Yet as adults, as writers, that's exactly what we do to ourselves: We place limits when we ought to allow ourselves the joy of play.

I suspect that time is a huge factor here. Who has the time to just play with dolls and let them do what they do?

Yup. I get it.

And yet, and *yet,* it is that very task that is essential, the daydreaming, the free write, the letting characters lead the way.

Hey Smarty Pants.
Line your pockets with *this*.

Want some great writing prompts based on neuroscience and guaranteed to jump you into writing flow? Watch the video series at www.writing-gym.com/brain.

The irony here is that in doing so, we ultimately *save* ourselves time in the revision process because we get a *firm* idea of who our character is and where she's going.

Believe me: Dealing with these types of questions when you believe yourself to be finished, only to find that your entire novel needs an overhaul is *not* a happy place to be. It's not untenable, but it's certainly discouraging, and many an author has given up when faced with that daunting task.

When is it time to invite the inner critic in for dinner?

We've talked about the creative phase as a distinct entity, which by logical extension means that the revision phase is also a distinct, separate entity.

People: These are dynamite and *fire!* Do not mix them up unless you want an explosion that will blow your writing ambitions right up.

As I mentioned, confusing the creation and revision phases is one of the *biggest* mistakes I see. It is not irreparable, but like a bad relationship mistake, sometimes the damage is difficult to undo or overcome.

Secret Sauce: The writing process is broken into two phases. Don't confuse the two!

That's because you've taught your neurons certain pathways that are difficult to undo once set.

I'm not just making this up for giggles and if you don't want to believe me, let's take a look at neuroscience.

This is your brain.

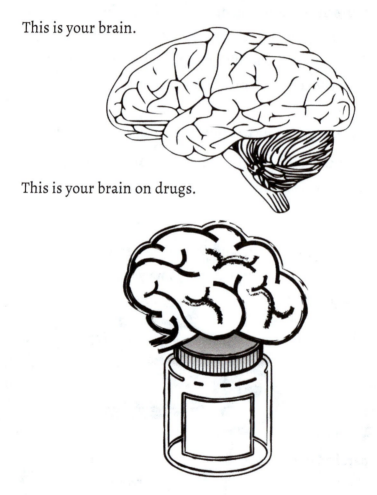

This is your brain on drugs.

Let's take a side trip. The Ancient Roman Poet Horace once said: "Mix a little foolishness with your prudence: It's good to be silly at the right moment." Remember what I said about creativity and play? What I did with the brain there was just plain silly. Absurdly silly, but let it be a model for you. You play in your way; maybe your brand of play is different from mine. The point is to allow yourself to frolic in the play, to get in touch with your inner child, and channel that energy into your writing.

And now you know that as a child, I had the same cheesy sense of humor I have as an adult. Send your condolences to my family.

Right. The brain.

CAUTION: SCIENCE AHEAD

If you're having trouble tapping into your creativity, take heart—no, literally.

Consider this: Your brain from its very origins was made to be in creative flow.

What am I talking about?

Think of a chocolate-covered cherry. It's got three main components: the gooey sweet stuff inside the cherry, the cherry, and the chocolate on top.

Your brain is a lot like this treat. The gooey inside is the oldest part of your brain, from an evolutionary standpoint. It is your reptilian brain, and

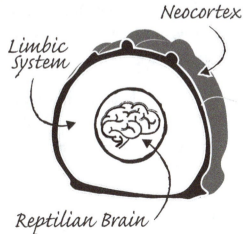

Neocortex

Limbic System

Reptilian Brain

it's in charge of survival. The cherry, as it were, is your limbic brain. It evolved later, and is the seat of emotion. Lastly is the delicious dark chocolate of thought: your neocortex.

Not only are these areas layered this way, but, like the rings on a tree, they show us the course of our own evolution. They also show us why and how sometimes we are our own worst enemy.

Play, creativity, being in creative flow, those are all seated in your limbic system. (The cherry, if you will.)

It is your thinking brain, your neocortex, that steps in and censors, that asks, "Will this work?" "Does that make sense?" "Am I getting enough symbolism in here?"

The work that I do with writers optimizes the balance between these two parts of your brain. In short, we work *with* the brain's flow and take into account when it's time to frolic, and when it's time to invite the inner critic in for dinner.

Knowing the difference between these two phases is an essential key not only to finishing a book, but finishing it in flow, in a happy place, instead of the drudgery that so many writers feel.

As you work, keep in mind that fundamentally, at your core, in the deepest part of your brain, of *you*, lives your creativity, the person you're meant to be.

But wait, there's more.

Did I mention there were *three* parts of the brain?

Ah yes, the reptilian brain. You've got a lizard in your head. (Only kidding. But seriously...)

As I said (wrote?), the reptilian brain is the oldest part of your brain (from an evolutionary standpoint), and it's *very* important to understand how it works.

Here's what you need to know: The reptilian brain is in charge of survival. See a lion? RUN. See a deer? Dinner. (It's very basic, this reptile brain.)

What I am talking about here is fight or flight. As you know, and as I mentioned above with the lion/deer thingie, fight or flight is your survival response to a stimulus.

In today's world, there aren't a whole lot of us running around being chased by lions or pursuing dinner in the forest on a daily basis. But, like our appendix, we're still stuck with the part, even if we've evolved not to need it—at least in the same way. (There are still, admittedly, dangers it is wise to run from.)

The *problem* is, sometimes this little bugger gets confused. It puts us into fight or flight mode when it's totally unwarranted. Have you ever yelled at your spouse and later said, "Honey, I'm sorry. I don't know what came over me."

You've been a victim of your brain.

Emotional Hijacking

"Emotional Hijacking" is a term coined by psychologist Daniel Goleman in his book *Emotional Intelligence: Why It Can Matter More Than IQ.*

Your brain is smart. (Duh!) It's set up so that if you're walking down the street, say, and a guy steps out of a doorway and draws a knife on you, you don't stand there thinking, "Could this guy be dangerous? Well, it *is* a small knife. And he kind of looks like cousin Harry, and *he's* a nice guy, so...Ooo, I wonder where he bought that hoodie. I've been looking for one in that color."

Chances are you'd be dead with a brain like that.

Now, if that guy stepped out of the doorway with a bag of groceries, the thought process above would be appropriate. Why? The guy's not posing a threat.

When your brain perceives a threat, it skips the rational brain (neocortex), and goes straight to an emotional evaluation (limbic system) and into fight or flight mode (reptilian brain). This is emotional hijacking.

Umm, Annalisa, this isn't a science book.

Yes, yes, I know. I am getting to the point.

This fight or flight response can be triggered in the writing process. Yup.

Don't believe me?

Think back to the time you left that free writing group, peeved, seething, ready to kick something and toss your manuscript.

Emotional hijacking.

Now, think of how your body reacted. Adrenaline rush. Raised heart rate. Inability to think clearly. Frantic.

Does that sound like the kind of mindset that's going to lead to good writing?

    A. Yes
    B. No
    C. Bananas

Good. You answered B. You've passed your first quiz.

Pat yourself on the back.

No. Really. Do it. Now.

So, if you see that it doesn't work, why would you keep going back to that group and expecting better results? Why not find something that optimizes the way your brain functions?

Braggy-brag moment

I have always been a writer and a teacher. I feel blessed to have had a vocation from the start and always to have known what I was born to do.

Before I was a full-time writing coach, I was a teacher and a professor. I've studied the learning process—specifically how the brain learns best—for over 20 years. I've taught every grade from preschool to graduate school (except eighth grade, which is just weird), and one of the most amazing moments—no matter the grade, no matter the subject—is that a-ha moment: the moment when someone understands something in a new way or acquires a new skill.

There are many great teachers out there, and I am proud to be among them. My own secret sauce to create as many a-ha moments as possible was to dig deep into how the brain works, so that I could tailor instruction to each student, to how he learned best. My use of neuroscientific principles in the classroom led to two Teacher of the Year nominations and, more importantly, a treasure of students who learned something in their time with me, and had a heck of a good time doing it.

That's what writing should be, *can* be. Is it work? Yes. But does it have to be hard? No.

Secret Sauce:
Use your brain...the right way.

Using your brain in the way it's intended to work is one of the most important tools a writer can have in his toolkit.

FINDING THE CONFIDENCE TO WRITE

Is My Writing Good Enough?

Let's talk about the writing mindset.

One question that keeps writers staring at the ceiling at 2 AM is: "Is my writing good enough?" This is something that plagues all writers, and I do mean *all* writers.

There are many pressures that writers place on themselves:

 Why is it taking me so long to finish my manuscript?
 I've been writing for so long. Haven't I gotten it right yet?
 What's the right way to write?

Why is it taking me so long to finish my manuscript?

Because fiction is *art*, and art takes *time*.

Consider the Sistine Chapel, painted by Michelangelo. It took four and a half years for him to complete that masterpiece, which—frankly, if you've seen the level of detail—you know it's astonishing he completed it so quickly.

What else?

The Washington Monument took thirty years to construct; *thirty full years.*

Let's think about more writing-related references.

It took Victor Hugo twelve years to write *Les Miserables* and Harper Lee spent two and a half years writing *To Kill a Mockingbird.*

Fiction writing is *art,* and art takes *time.* Completing your manuscript is not going to happen overnight, not because there's something wrong with you, but because you are an *artist.*

My writing mentor, award-winning author of *In the Time of the Butterflies* (among others) Julia Alvarez, wasn't the first one to say it, but she *was* the first one to say it to *me:* Being a writer is 90% applying butt to chair.

I've been writing for so long. Haven't I gotten it right yet?

We learned to write at an early age, right? Many of us, very early on in elementary school, were writing some type of stories as part of our school curriculum. Storytelling is something we've been doing for a long time and, therefore, is something we've been getting feedback on for a long time.

Ergo, we've had a really long time to be overly critical of ourselves, or to let feedback that wasn't helpful seep in and become that recording that we tell ourselves about the world and our own writing.

Here's the real deal: Your elementary school teachers, your middle school teachers, and probably even your high school teachers meant well. I hope for you that somewhere along the way, you found someone who really understood story, who took you under his or her wing and really worked with you on the principles of writing.

That said, there are many of us who didn't have that mentor. Now, before we get all blamey-blamey on our teachers, the school board, and the entire educational system in America going down the tubes, and...

Take a deep breath. Remember that your English teachers' job wasn't necessarily to teach you about the the finer points of how to construct a story. In fact, they might not have even known those things for themselves. They had other objectives. They were there to teach you about syntax, or the different parts of speech, or how to respond to Dostoyevsky.

They had other objectives that were set forth for them by the state, by their local school board, by national standards, whatever the case may be, but their objectives weren't about the art of quality writing.

Not to go all *Frozen* on you (because that is *so* 2013), but *let it go*.

We all have a story to tell about something that happened in the fourth grade, or the eighth grade, where someone didn't believe in our writing, and that's ok. It isn't personal. Your teacher had a lot to do—I can tell you that *for sure*—and their *teaching* objective didn't match the *learning* objective you set for yourself on this amazing journey to the Land of Published Authors.

It's ok. Put it in your locker. Slam the door. Walk away. You've graduated. It's time to move on.

What's the right way to write?

Look people, let's just clear this one up once and for all.

There is no right way to get this thing called writing done. There are more efficient ways. There are ways that are more faithful to principles of craft. There are ways that are a better fit for you and your brain, and the way you think. But there is no "right" way.

It's ok to write a quick first draft and spend a long time revising.

Flip that around.

It's ok to spend a long time writing a first draft and less time revising.

When it comes to the "right" way to write, we've got a true case of separate but equal, and the only determining factor is *what works best for you.*

While we're talking about flipping things around, let's consider flipping our point of view. No, not the point of view of our novel (though we'll get to that in the clarity section), our *own* point of view, how we see ourselves and our writing.

One is the loneliest number

What happens to us writers? We writers spend a lot of time in solitude; we're alone working away on our novels, and during that solitary time our worries magnify. There's something about that solitude that just makes worry churn, and because we're the only ones talking to ourselves, giving ourselves feedback, that small problem becomes bigger and bigger and bigger.

It's important to notice and recognize that this process is happening to us: that we spend so much time alone with our craft, and that maybe our vision is a little bit skewed. Things are a little bit out of proportion, and we might be seeing things through a lens that isn't necessarily accurate because we're too close to it, for example.

Secret Sauce: Breathing deeply ultimately leads to easier writing.

Keep this idea in mind, be gentle with yourself, and take a deep breath. Really. Take a deep breath.

Remember your brain?

Deep breathing increases oxygen and blood flow to the brain, which in turn creates fertile ground for quality thinking and creativity. As I mentioned, in my work with writers we spend a lot of time working through exercises specifically targeted to enhance brain functioning and to create fertile ground for creativity.

This kind of supportive community is another asset that helps writers to break free from the trap of self doubt. Breaking free from the solitary act of writing, and becoming a part of the *right* community, can do wonders for your self image as a writer.

There's a U in the middle of Truth

Did you ever notice there's a "u" standing in the middle of "truth"?

Now, not to go all Nietzsche or Kant on you, but here's my philosophy: I believe in facing your truth; facing *the* truth, and really embracing it, for better or for worse.

I love to be silly. (Have you caught on to that one yet?) You'll hear me tell knock-knock jokes and ridiculous things like that, but I'm also really *serious* about facing my own truths.

That means being honest with myself about my shortcomings *and* my strengths.

Why?

I feel that there's power in looking at things from a standpoint of self-honesty. Once we've admitted our truth, we can deal with it. If, for example, we're ignoring the fact that our solitude is impacting us, then we're never going to get to the root of that problem.

What does this mean for writers?

The truth here is to accept the writer that you are here, now, today. As a writer, this process might mean thinking about things like: Maybe you're not the best writer you could be today—and that's ok. That might just be the truth.

Maybe solitude or the writing group you're in now aren't serving you and you need a quality experience. Maybe your writing isn't where you want it to be. Maybe you compare yourself to someone else and think, "I wish I could be that person." But you are the writer that you are, and that's exactly the person that you are supposed to be right now.

Like your manuscript, you are a work in progress. You bought this book to move your writing forward. You will continue to grow, change, and advance as you put energy into the effort to do so. So, accept the writer that you are, and congratulate yourself for taking the small step of buying this book to improve yourself as of today. Then move forward to find the kind of long term solutions that will help you to become the writer you want to be, and to flourish.

There's a monster under the bed

In the comic strip, five-year-old Calvin and his stuffed tiger, Hobbes, spend a lot of time obsessing about the monster under the bed. It's humorous, it's charming, and it's reminiscent.

It connects us, the readers, to the innocence of our childhood fears...

And yet—

We writers lie awake staring at the ceiling, wrestling with our demons. We might as well call that the monster under the bed.

There's nothing quaint about fear, no matter one's age. The monsters we writers face are just as imaginary and just as *real*, as the ones of our childhood.

One of the biggest monsters? The monster of comparison.

Here's another shift in point of view that you can make as you think about your writing: When we compare ourselves to others, we often talk about changing, being something *else*. As a writer, what would happen if you looked for ways to *improve* versus change?

When we compare ourselves to others, we're missing the unique gifts that we bring to the table. Hemingway is Hemingway. Had he compared himself to Tolstoy, we might have lost something, right?

We're all unique, and I don't mean that in some sort of woo-woo, fuzzy, washed out way. I'm serious. You have something that you can share in the world that is yours, and that is a wonderful, *wonderful* gift, and I hope you can come to a point where you can really accept that.

Writing is growth. There's never a moment where you arrive and you say, "That's it! I am an amazing writer!" We're always moving forward and questioning; it's part of the process. Keep in mind that there's always going to be this ebb and flow, and that's just part of the process—it might

Secret Sauce:
Writers rarely feel like they've arrived. It's always a process of growth.

make our stomachs upset sometimes—but we *can* look at the truth, accept that the situation just *is*.

This vulnerability is the nature of being a writer. It's the nature of exposing your inner thoughts. It's the nature of not only exposing those inner thoughts, but putting them out into the world for other people to look at, judge, and potentially reject.

The bravery to put one's work out into the world is certainly something to be celebrated, and in my work with writers, we do just that every day: Celebrate the wins, big and small.

Secret disclosure: I've always been a bit of a ham. There have been *many* times where people didn't "get it," rolled their eyes at me, or told me I was simply not funny. (They were totally wrong, am I right? Ok, moving on.)

Yet here I am writing this silly, goofy, fun, serious book on writing.

Some people will pick it up and roll their eyes. Some will buy it. Some will read it and love it.

Why did I do it this way? I could have written a very academic piece, slapped a Latin title on it, and called it done. So, why this book in this way?

Because this book is about *my* view on writing, about the approach I take in my work with writers; it's about *my* passion for craft and helping writers to become authors. It is, in essence, *me*.

Let's face it: There are a million books out there on writing. But there's only one me.

And, at the end of the day, there's only one *you*, and *you've* got an important story to tell too.

Getting that story out, helping you to see wonderful you, that's my passion.

Let's make that happen.

To err is human

Here's another truth: Failure is part of the writing process.

We sometimes have interesting philosophies around failure; we don't often look at it as the opportunity it can be.

Look, I know it doesn't feel great to fail.

The issue, as I see it, is that once we get to a certain age, we're no longer used to failure. When we were very young, failure was part of the daily routine and we used it to help us learn.

Think about you the baby. There was a moment of time—and I'm sure Mom or Dad told some great stories about this— where you were learning to walk and you fell many times. It was cute and your parents took videos or pictures; they called their parents to tell them about it.

Falling was a natural part of the process. Nobody said, "Oh my goodness, he's never going to learn to walk. What a failure this baby is."

Instead, they held your hand, guided you through what didn't work, and moved you toward what did work until you were able to do it on your own.

(Sounds a lot like what a good coach does to me!)

Secret Sauce:
Failure is *part* of the learning *process*.

Still don't believe me?

Think about when you learned to form letters. It was so cute and your parents put your little notes on their refrigerator, back- wards and

upside letters, made-up spellings and all. They didn't tell you you were a failure and would never learn to spell or write. (They were wise, your parents.) They recognized the journey.

That same forgiveness that our parents had as we went through the various phases of early childhood we also had for ourselves because we didn't know better.

We hadn't learned to equate falling with failure, and failure as bad. That's a construct that came much, much later, one that now darkens our writing doors.

What would happen if we changed our point of view? What if we said, "Yeah, I'm going to fail, *and* I'm going to learn something."?

The more that we can approach failure in that way, the less anxiety and the fewer stomachaches we will have, and the more progress we'll make. This change in perspective is about being gentle with yourself and attempting, to the extent possible, not to take those setbacks personally.

Look, we all hate failure. We're all afraid of failing. It never goes away. However, we *can* learn to walk with that fear, dance with it even. I believe this wholeheartedly, as it forms the foundation of what I do every day in the Writing Gym.

Oh, Doubting Thomas

Maybe you still don't believe me. It's ok. You're not the first writer I've met who wants to cling to that fear. It's got a powerful hold.

The thing is, my dear fellow writer, we *all* fail. Even when we've been at this for a lifetime, after we've had monumental success, we still fail. Because there are still lessons to learn.

Still don't believe me? Fine. Fine. Fine.

(You're awfully stubborn, you know.)

Let us sit at the feet of those who wrote before us.

Many of you know about the Writing Gym podcast where we interview best-selling authors, agents, publishers, and editors about their writing tips and tricks.

When we were talking with *New York Times* best-seller Bob Burg, he told us a story about what had happened with the title of his and John David Mann's book. What I want to point out is that this is a multiple best-selling author, an exceedingly successful businessman—this guy knows what he's talking about—yet he still made a mistake, had a failure with choosing a book title and I want you to see how he and John turned that failure into a lesson.

> After *The Go-Giver* we wrote a follow-up that was more application-based called *Go-Givers Sell More*. That one sold very well, so not an issue there. But then the publisher asked us to do another parable: a follow-up to *The Go-Giver.*
>
> So, we did one called *It's Not About You*, which, to us or anyone who had read *The Go-Giver*...should know that it came from Law Number Three, the Law of Influence (your influence is determined by how abundantly you place other people's interests...so on and so forth).
>
> We thought that would be a natural follow-up, and it would even be an appealing title for those who hadn't read the first book.
>
> We were wrong.

People didn't buy the book, and they didn't buy it in droves, which was amazing to us.

We couldn't understand why, because the people who bought it said, "This is as good as *The Go-Giver*," and so forth and so on.

But I was speaking to one person and we're just talking about how some books sell, some don't...and he said, "you know, Bob, it's interesting: a book called *It's Not About You*." He said, "You know, if I was looking at it and I didn't know you, I'd look at the title and I'd say, 'Well if it's not about me, why would I want it?'"

And that made pretty good sense.

But there was also something else: One reason for the sales of *The Go-Giver* is that it's a gift book. People feel very comfortable giving a book to someone with the title *The Go-Giver* because what are you saying? It's like you're saying, "Hey this is you, you're a go-giver."

Think about it. You're going to give this book as a gift called "It's not about you." *Hmm, what's this person trying to tell me?* It's like giving someone a bottle of Scope mouthwash.

I love what Bob says here. I mean, this is a man who has the foreword to his book written by Arianna Huffington, which is no small feat. This book is recommended by Spencer Johnson, who wrote the book *Who Moved My Cheese?* among others, and yet: He made a mistake; he had a moment of failure in choosing a title.

If you still think that you're alone on the failure train, let's have a chat with my author pal John David Mann.

If you head over to Mr. Mann's website, you'll see two full pages of published books, including *New York Times* best-sellers. This is a man who has written not one *New York Times* best-seller, but several, and won multiple literary awards. This is a writer we would all aspire to be, right? Someone we would think would have it rock solid, tied up, could publish anything, anywhere, any time?

Let's hear what he has to say about writing failures and flops.

> I just finished a book: a parable about a young boy who's in trouble, a fourteen-year-old kid who, once his father leaves, his life is going downhill, he's getting in trouble, getting in fights, major suffering, angry at the world, and he crosses paths with a crusty old diner chef that turns out to be a retired award-winning chef, and he goes to work for this guy in the kitchen.
>
> Life learning ensues, and it's a parable.
>
> My agent has taken it now to over forty publishers, all of whom said no. And this is the first time this has happened for me. I've got a book—I think it's a good book—and nobody's publishing it.
>
> So I say that just because rejection and barriers and brick walls are a fact of life that don't go away, even once you're successful and have what I've got—I've published about two dozen books, two million copies, two dozen foreign languages copies. I can't get anybody to publish this book.

You heard it from the horse's mouth. Sorry, John, you're not a horse...uh, what I mean is: I can't say it any better than he did.

If you're going to write anything on a sticky note and place it on your writing desk, quote John David Mann.

"Rejection and barriers and brick walls are a fact of life." – John David Mann

So, what is the truth here?

You are going to fail.

And it's ok.

You're going to *fail*.

And it's *ok*.

Secret Sauce:
"Rejection and barriers and brick walls are a fact of life."
John David Mann

It's part of the process. Beyond that, you don't know what's going on behind the scenes. So many, many times, we submit something for publication, get a rejection back, and we think that it's all about us.

We think, "Oh, I must not be a very good writer," or, "I must have the characters all wrong," or, "I did something wrong with my query letter." Whatever it is, we take it upon ourselves.

And it may very well be about us, the quality of the story...OR

It might be about something else entirely.

Just like a job interview, or any other time that we put ourselves out there in the world, we don't know what's going on behind the scenes. It might not be the right time for the piece that you submitted. It might not be the right market. Agents and publishers have a lot of inside information on what's hot right now, and the winds change in each genre from moment to moment.

Really, let's be fair with the agents and publishers; they're all trying to make guesses too about what the next big thing is.

Harry Potter is a great example of that. How many times did *Harry Potter* get rejected? And then it ended up as a multi-billion dollar industry.

They guessed wrong; they guessed the market wouldn't support that story, and in fact, it did—in spades. Agents are just scrambling to look for the next thing, and we don't know what their projections and guesses are.

So, why should we take rejection personally? It's not personal and, at the end of the day, if it *is* personal, if someone doesn't accept your story, they think you're a jerk, or not cool, or too cool— you don't want to work with them anyway. That would just be a nightmare.

If you've ever been in a work relationship with someone who it is not easy to get along with, then you know that that's just not your thing. You don't want to be there. Just say, "Thank you for the rejection," and move on to the next thing.

When to invite the inner critic in for dinner

All right, here comes a big one. We're going to talk about that inner critic.

From an early age, we're trained to look for what's wrong, to focus on what needs to be fixed. Our teachers and parents were well-intentioned (one hopes), but during the training process called growing up, it's pointed out to us often what it is that we need to fix, what we need to do better, how to hold the fork... you get the idea.

Our parents are training us to survive in the world, but the process also trains our brain to start looking for what's wrong.

Let's take a moment to give the inner critic her due.

We writers frequently speak of the inner critic as the enemy. She certainly *can* be an enemy, especially at times when we're trying to be hyper-creative and nothing's flowing the way we want it to.

But let's keep this in mind: The inner critic is there for a reason. She actually serves a purpose for us: She protects us from that which might otherwise harm us. This is important: That's why she's there; that's why we have her.

So, let's turn that beat around and take a moment to be grateful for the inner critic. Knowing when to say "Thank you" and "No thanks, not now" to the inner critic are two really important steps on the journey to being a writer who finishes books.

(You do know you can't *publish* a book if you don't *finish* writing it, right?)

So, knowing how to have a *relationship* with your inner critic is vital. One of the best skills I believe a writer can possess is to know *how* and *when* the inner critic gets invited in for dinner, and when the invitation is politely declined.

Winning the Lottery

Every year at Christmas, Santa flies down from the North Pole in his little sleigh just to fill my stocking with goodies. When he's not busy filling it with lotion and makeup samples, he throws in some scratch tickets.

We sit around passing the coins and scratching the gray goop off the little lottery tickets to match snowflakes with silver bells hoping to get rich. Every couple of years someone wins 40 bucks and we all cheer, and every year, someone wins two bucks here or five bucks there.

Imagine if we're scratching away and someone wins a GRAND PRIZE—$1000, $5000 or the $10,000 jackpot. Sure, it's cool to win, but how much *more* cool is it that it's the one time in a whole calendar year that we ever play a scratch ticket. Bingo! Hazzah! Winner!

Many writers treat their writing life like my once-a-year scratch tickets. They submit every now and then *hoping* and wishing themselves *luck*—as if publishing were a lottery ticket that relies on chance.

Writing is *not* the lottery. As we've seen, it's an art and a skill.

So why do writers treat writing like the lottery?

> *Knock Knock*
> Who's There?
> *Inner Critic*

If I submit every now and then, and I'm rejected, no big deal. I'm not *really* invested.

HOWEVER (Did you see how big that "however" was?) if I work and work and work, and *then* submit and I'm rejected—that hurts.

Ouch. Sting. Burn.

I worked SO hard—all that effort for nothing.

Remember the inner critic's job? To *protect* you. Do you want to feel that pain? No. Of course not.

So here's what the inner critic whispers in your ear:

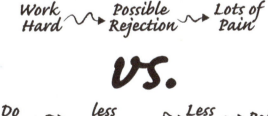

She's well-intentioned, really, she is, but often, like the babysitter who bribes the kid with candy to stop crying, she does not always have our long-term interests at heart. (See emotional hijacking.)

The methods to circumvent this pain-avoiding process are paramount to your writing success! I highly recommend you find a writing program that addresses how to deal with your fear in a productive way to lead you to publishing success.

Sure, you can learn about character arcs and point of view all the livelong day, but if you're not addressing your brain's needs, your brain will block you time and again.

Yes, the key to the writing life is butt in chair (thanks again, Julia), but there's also a mental game, creating the stamina and the strategies that lead to success.

Overlooking this *very* important step is one of the biggest mistakes I see writers make.

Instead they get bogged down in what they call writer's block. (Guilty party: inner critic.) Many writers allow themselves to stay there for weeks, months, even *years*.

They waste time not knowing *what* to write or *how* to write it, or researching the same thing every which way to Novel-Never-Written Land.

Is that what you want for yourself?

No?

Keep reading.

What if Nobody Likes me?

Ah yes, rejection.

Perhaps the greatest fear of all.

We're afraid of rejection—of course we are. There is so much rejection that comes with being a writer. Even if you never submit your writing for publication (which I know isn't going to be true for you or you wouldn't be holding this book), there are still so many other kinds of rejection.

We talked about things that happened to us in school. Maybe you've shared your writing with a loved one and they didn't like it, or they've said they really liked it and you're pretty clear that they didn't.

We're afraid of big failures too: You've written an entire book, and you can't get it published. Think about John David Mann.

What would have happened if John had given up? Well, there were many books he wrote and published after *The Recipe*—which, by the way was eventually published.

Will that be the happy ending for everyone?

Nope.

The point is, he never would have gotten to success if he'd let rejection stand in the way.

So the thing about being a writer—and here's the truth—if you want to publish not once, not twice, but many, many times and be the very best writer that you can, you need to push through that fear. It's natural to be afraid, but if you don't push through it, you're never going to achieve your writing goals.

Big Important Strategy

That's great, Annalisa, but *how*? *How* do I get over all of these fears, and the anxiety, and staring at the ceiling, and the monsters under my bed and...

Breathe.

No, really.

Remember what I said about oxygen to the brain?

Take three deep breaths, and then set your eyes on your goals.

You should have your goals in mind at all times. Goal setting and accountability are two of the absolute must-have components of a quality writing program, one that helps you to keep on writing and to finish a publishable manuscript.

Your goals are your touchstones all along the way. "Why am I doing this?" "Why am I getting up at 5 AM to write?" "Why am I staying up until eleven to write?"

This is what I want to do; these are my goals.

Keep coming back to those goals and pushing past the inner critic. It's difficult. It's uncomfortable. You're growing and changing and that hurts.

Why are we doing it?

We have these goals.

FINDING THE TIME
TO WRITE

So...I don't want to be a doomsayer, but there is a big consequence of not dealing with your fear. Writers come to me all the time and they say that they struggle with finding time to write. If you're a member of my Facebook group for writers, "Write to PUBLISH," then I'm sure that you've seen our poll asking what's hard about writing now. "Finding time to write" is not just the most popular choice, the number of writers who choose "finding the time to write" as their number one struggle doubles all of the other choices.

Finding time to write is clearly a big problem for writers. While it is true that we have busy lives: kids and jobs and cars and things that we need to take care of, (here comes another truth:) it's really easy to procrastinate that which we fear, right?

If we think something will cause us pain, in other words fear, it's easy to avoid that thing. It's easy to find other tasks to do.

It's easy to turn on the TV or clean the kitchen, or take our dog for a walk, or whatever else it is that needs to be done—because we're afraid. We have all of those fears that we just talked about and we choose to do other things.

So, it's not *really* that we don't have time to write. Not usually. Nine times out of ten it's that we didn't make the time because we are afraid.

Secret Sauce:
Often when we say we have no time to write, the real problem is not making time because we're afraid.

How are we going to combat this?

We're going to have a shift in our mindset.

In order to find your best writer, you're going to have to make some shifts—not only in the way you see things, but also in the way you behave.

I want to tell you a story that somebody told me in college about the two jars. Maybe you've heard this one before.

RECIPE FOR SUCCESS

Ingredients

    2 large Mason jars

    4 baby-fist sized rocks

    4 cups tiny pebbles separated into half

    8 cups sand divided in half

Directions Jar 1:

    1) Place 4 cups sand in the jar.

    2) Place 2 cups pebbles.

    3) Place the rocks.

Do the rocks fit? No.

Directions Jar 2:

    1) Place the rocks in the jar.

    2) Place 2 cups pebbles.

    3) Place 4 cups sand in the jar.

Did it all fit? YES!

Yay. We filled a jar. Happy dance. Woo hoo! Yes. High Fives all around. Cue the celebration music.

Hmm. Clearly filling the jar was not the point of exercise.

No, of course not.

The rocks represent the most important things in your life, the things that need to be put in first. The pebbles, of course, are the secondary things—your obligations. The sand is all the things we have to do, but aren't really life priorities—things like cleaning the toilet or washing the car. They must be done, but they're not the fulfilling, meaningful stuff in life.

This illustration shows that if you put in the obligations, the things that you feel like you *have* to do first, then there is going to be no more room for the big rocks at the top. It won't all fit in that jar.

HOWEVER, (Hmm, look at that large font again.) if you put the big rocks in first—the most important things in your life go in that jar first—and then you put in the things that are pretty important to you, and then you fill in the things that you're obligated to do, everything fits into the jar.

So, what does this mean for your writing?

If writing is most important thing in your life—which, if you're reading this book, I'm guessing that it is—then it has to be the very first thing that goes into your day.

Now, I'm not saying that you need to start your day by writing; it doesn't have to happen first thing in the morning. But it *does* need to be the first priority. You need to make that space in your life first.

Where's the writing space in your life? When is that going to happen every single day?

Once you've committed to make writing the most important thing and set a plan in motion to make it happen, then finding the quality support and the accountability that make writing happen is one of the most important steps you can take for yourself.

When you've faced the fear—put that big rock into the jar first to say—"I'm taking a stand. Writing is important to me—I'm going to make this happen in my life;" when you continue to do that *every day*, to say, "Today I made writing the most important thing in my life," you'll feel so empowered in your writing that it *will* get done.

Getting into a practice that helps you to move from not good enough requires a firm decision and the support to make writing continue to happen. You need the kind of support that works you through the rough patches, keeps you dedicated, and helps you to hold the commitments you've made to yourself. Once you find that place, that question: "Is my writing good enough?" won't even matter anymore.

Promise.

Hey Smarty Pants.
Line your pockets with *this.*

Download the accountability calendar used in the Writing Gym Accountability Sessions and the extra BONUS: Tips on battling procrastination. www.writing-gym. com/accountability

If books could whisper in your ear

While we're talking about finding the time to write, I want to mention one more activity that is important to find time to do: reading.

Please! Please please please please!!! (Do you see how I am begging you?) Do not take that plaque that says "John Smith, Writer" and even *think* about hanging it on your door unless you are making time to *read*!

I don't mean just read the back of the cereal box in the morning. I mean, read *widely*. You write sci fi? Great. By all means, read *lots* of sci fi. (It will help you to know what's already been done, what's marketable, what the conventions of your genre are and so on.)

But, please, (don't make me beg again!) read everything. Read crime fiction, and Victorian Literature, and Twain, and the *New York Times*, and *MAD Magazine*.

Read. It. *ALL!*

Don't believe me?

Ok, ok, ok. Make me pull in the *big time* experts again. Fine.

Secret Sauce: You can't be a good writer if you're not an avid reader.

As I was writing my first novel in my early 20s, Stephen King's book *On Writing* changed my writing life. (Thank you, Mr. King.) I don't have to tell you how prolific ole Steve is—he's got so many published works on his website, I can't even count that high.

This guy is as full of books as he is of wisdom on writing.

Oh look, you've got mail:

To: StubbornReader@storytellingforpantsers.com
From: *The* Stephen King
Re: The relationship between reading and writing

If you don't have time to read, you don't have the time (or the tools) to write. Simple as that.

Sincerely,
Stephen King

So, there you have it. Don't believe me, but please do believe Stephen King. Reading is *essential* to writing. Besides, if you want people to buy your book, you should be supporting your fellow authors and buying theirs.

What goes around comes around. Karma and all that.

Hey Smarty Pants.
Line your pockets with *this*.

Curious what books are on my nightstand? Download my top ten book list at www.writing-gym. com/readbooks

HOW TO FIND THE KIND OF SUPPORT YOU NEED TO HELP YOU BE YOUR VERY BEST WRITER

Feedback

The second most prevalent complaint I hear from writers over in "Write to PUBLISH" is about not getting the right kind of feedback.

Feedback is one of the most precious commodities to the writing life. Though quality feedback cannot be undervalued in the writing life, it continues to be a major frustration for so many writers.

They often ask me:

- What kind of feedback do I need?
- Where can I get it?
- What does quality feedback even look like?

I think so much of the confusion comes from the variety of effectiveness of resources that are out there, and the wealth of negative experiences writers have had with the majority of writing groups available.

No pressure or anything

Quality feedback is vital to a publishable manuscript and yet it's so difficult to find. No wonder writers feel anxiety about feedback. So much is at stake and it's so difficult to find the right match.

Secret Sauce:
Quality feedback is vital to a publishable manuscript.

When writers get the feedback cycle wrong, well, I've seen writers take years off from writing, give up, drop writing all together, and never go back to it.

I'm sure if I started a support group, we could all share our Feedback Horror Stories...

"There was this one time that..."

[Ok, fine, let's start a thing: tweet me your #FeedbackHorrorStory @annalisaparent. Ooo, this is going to be fun.]

I know *you* would never do this, because you're the kind of writer who was smart enough to pick up this book, but *many* writers commit this deadly sin of writing: They think anyone can give them feedback.

Let's play imagine again, ok?

Imagine you wake up tomorrow morning and realize that your lifelong dream is to play hockey in the NHL. What do you do to reach that dream?

Well, you know, a professional coach is expensive, and the ice time at the rink? Highway robbery!

So, you're just going to fill your back yard with the water from the hose and wait for it to freeze. Meanwhile, your neighbor's best friend's cousin knows a guy who used a date a gal who was a cheerleader with the wife of a guy who was on a pro hockey team. So, your neighbor is going to give you skating lessons. Great.

You *do* have that honest friend in your life, don't you? The one who comes in and says, "Oh honey, this ain't going to work..."

Call your honest friend on the phone. Do it now.

Are you going to make it into the NHL by skating in the back yard with some guy who knows a little about how to stand upright on a pair of skates?

No?

Well, guess what?

ENTER: Honest Friend

If you want to publish, you're looking at the NHL of the writing world. If the neighbor isn't the right coach to help you meet your NHL aspirations, why do you think your sister who got an A in high school English 10 years ago, or the guy down the street, is the right person to give you feedback on your novel?

Lean in. I'm going to tell you a secret.

Secret Sauce:
Your friends and family are 99.99999% guaranteed not to give you the kind of feedback you need to get your novel to publishable.

Your friends and family are 99.99999% guaranteed not to give you the kind of feedback you need to get your novel to publishable.

I know, you *think* they're being honest with you. They've *told* you they're being honest with you. And they're full of...

Well, anyway.

The thing is: Your friends are about as likely to give you honest feedback on your book as they are to give you honest feedback on your choice of life partner and how you're raising your kids. These are the kinds of conversations that break down relationships.

If you're lucky, a loved one *might* say, "I really liked it, but I don't understand why the main character was kissing that tree at the end." That's about the height of quality you're going to get from loved ones.

Why? They love you. They don't want to hurt you. Also, they know you so well, it's likely hard for them to separate *you* from your book.

My friends think I am hilarious (of course they *all* do), so they're going to think my book is hilarious. They love me, and they will see the things they love about me in my book. That's sweet—but it's not helpful to bring my book to clarity.

Did I hire an editor for this book? You bet your sweet bippy. And I'm an *editor*.

Did I ask my friends to read this book pre-publication? Nope. My mom? Nope.

(My dog *did* read it, but she was having a bout of insomnia, and I don't think that really counts. Either that or she just fell asleep on the printed manuscript…)

Moving on.

Most importantly, as your loved ones are concerned, they're rarely qualified. Are they trained to give feedback on story structure?

Reader Feedback vs. Writing Feedback

If you're looking for *reader* feedback, friends and family *can* be helpful. Readers give this kind of feedback: *I liked it. I didn't like it.* (Think "third grade book report" or "Amazon review"—speaking of which it's never too early to give *Storytelling for Pantsers* an amazing five-star Amazon review.)

If you're looking for content editing, the kind that tells you what isn't working in your writing and why…well, let's take a little quiz, shall we?

Sharpen your pencils, here we go.

1) If you want bread, you go to a _____.
2) If you have a broken leg, you go to a_____.
3) If you want content editing, you go to a _____.

Answer Key: 1) Baker; 2) Doctor; 3) Content Editor

How did you do? 100%?

Good. Now, are you ready to make that a lifestyle?

Are you ready to take your writing seriously enough, take yourself as a writer seriously enough, to bring it to the right professional to help move your writing forward instead of relying on your neighbor's best friend's cousin who knows a guy who used a date a gal who was a cheerleader with the wife of a guy who did an internship at a publishing house in college?

The thing is: Feedback is complicated. Mastering your craft to the equivalent of the NHL takes time, work, tears, sweat, determination, and the right kind of coaching.

Writing, like any other skill, is one which has its better teaching techniques and its poor teaching techniques.

Secret Sauce: Reader feedback and writing feedback are not the same. Don't confuse them.

Now I am not going to mention any names, but I have seen people hang their editing sign out, and they've never published, have no experience, or they're a Jack of 86 million trades.

I'm not saying there aren't talented people out there. I can walk and chew bubble gum at the same time. I'm just saying be wary. Your manuscript is valuable and you don't want just anybody mucking around in it.

What am I talking about? Well, let's hunker down into the trenches of what you need when it comes to quality feedback.

Whether you're working with an editor or you're looking for a group to give you feedback, the attributes of a quality experience are the same.

First, let's take a look at what you *don't* want. You may have experienced some of these (remember #FeedbackHorrorStory). You may have sensed that these experiences didn't work without really understanding why.

I'm going to help you to fill in some of those blanks, then talk about how you can find the right kind of feedback to help move your writing *forward*.

QUALITIES OF
WRONG FEEDBACK

Wrong source

As we have already discussed, many people get their feedback from the wrong source.

Your neighbor, the guy who will "edit" your manuscript for free or a couple hundred bucks, these are all bad choices.

If you're saying, "Wait, why? Isn't

Secret Sauce:
When it comes to quality feedback, asking friends and family is a big no-no.

that good enough?" please re-read the previous section, and then ask yourself:

1) Is "good enough" what I think will get me published?
2) Is "good enough" the kind of book I want my name on?

DANGER: Ego Ahead

Many writers join those free community writing groups and hang out amongst other struggling writers looking to get their name out into the world. Is it nice to have camaraderie? Sure. Are these the best people to give you feedback on your work? Probably not.

Why? These free peer-to-peer writing groups often work in the same way: You write a chapter or so, submit X pages, everyone is supposed to read it and offer critique.

First of all, few people read it, and even fewer people actually do the critique.

Once you convene for discussion, it's highly likely your fellow writers are comparing their work to yours.

Who cares?

Well, you *should* care. I've heard this story over and over and *over* again. Fellow writers in a group feel threatened by the talent a writer exhibits or the idea they came up with or...heaven knows what. Then what happens?

Remember that thingie about fight or flight and what the brain does when it feels threatened? Well, here it's going to fight. And you're going to end up the victim of some inexplicable attacks.

(Has this happened to you?)

Sometimes these attacks might be writing specific, but many times they are not. They often become personal very quickly. I talked with one writer who left a writing group because she was perpetually being teased (by a guy she was sure was jealous of her writing) for the brand of laptop she'd purchased. I've seen writers kicked out of a group inexplicably, mocked for lifestyle choices, or other things that have nothing to do with their writing.

All of this behavior stems from the green-eyed monsters of jealousy and comparison.

You may have had this kind of experience. I am here to tell you—there are no circumstances in which that kind of feedback is helpful. *None. Not one.*

Secret Sauce: If you get the wrong kind of feedback, you may end up the victim of the green-eyed monsters of jealousy and comparison.

Yet it happens all the time to writers in peer feedback groups.

Ego gets in the way.

I've been on the red carpet at Hollywood premiers; I've worked in television; and I've worked with best-selling authors—and here is one thing I can assure you is true: Beginners have a chip on their shoulder. Of course they do! They're afraid they're going to fail. Established people in any industry have a certain humility about them; they know they're successful. They know that could change at any moment, and they know how much work it took to get there.

Do you want to be getting advice from people who feel like they are your competitors, who feel that your success represents their failure? Does that sound like the place to get quality feedback to you?

It has been my experience, and I hear it from other writers all the time: When it comes to these free or peer-to-peer feedback groups, getting poor feedback is more the norm than is getting quality feedback.

Secret Sauce: The effects of getting the wrong type of feedback can be damaging and long term.

The effects of these experiences can be damaging and long term. I've had writers come to me in tears, writers who had this kind of experience and didn't write again for years or, worse yet, never wrote again.

Look, I don't want that to happen to you. I want you to find the quality feedback that will lead to growth and publication as many times as you want it.

Is that what you want for yourself? Is the free writing group worth it? Think carefully if that's something you want to have happen in your life. Are you willing to be attacked personally?

Does that work for you and your writing?

Unqualified for the job

There are certain attributes our critiquers should have. First of all, they should have some experience in our genre. Each genre has its own conventions, and not knowing them can be a fatal mistake for feedback.

Have you ever been in a feedback group where someone says, "Well, I've never read anything in this genre, but..." This is not a quality feedback experience. Can this person give you *reader* feedback? Sure. *I liked it. I didn't like. I hate your main character. I like your main character.* That's it. That's the limit.

If that's the kind of feedback you want, by all means, proceed.

If you think you're going to get quality *writing* feedback from that scenario, I am sorry to have to tell you that the feedback this person is going to give you is more likely to mess with your head than to help your writing in any meaningful way.

Look, I am not going to give you advice on buying Italian sports cars...because I know *nothing* about Italian sports cars. I can give you some cursory advice: Red might be nice. Or, I heard yellow sports cars get more tickets than any other color.

Is that helpful to someone in the market for a car? Probably not. They want to know about horsepower and transmissions—and, well, all kinds of things I don't know about.

When you ask people writing and reading outside your genre, you are asking Annalisa for Italian sports car advice.

How much do you *really* care about your writing future?

Here are the outside limitations of these kinds of groups:

- They can lend a (limited) helping hand—encouragement to finish, perhaps.
- They can give a good tip—maybe they read a good article on writing.
- They can share a pointer in their *specific* area of expertise, e.g. dialogue.

That's it.

Let's go back to the Land of Hockey Analogies.

Hockey Skate
(no toe pick)   Figure Skate
(toe pick)

After about a decade of figure skating, I played hockey for the first time. Now, if you've ever figure skated, you know how useful the toe pick is for stopping, for working spins, and other tricks. And if you've ever played hockey, you know that a hockey skate does *not* have a toe pick.

So, there I am out on the ice with my stick moving the puck toward the goal, having a heck of a good time. Someone charges me from the left, and I want to stop suddenly to change direction. What do I do? Reach for the toe pick.

End result? Well, that's how I found out that it doesn't hurt, in all that gear, to do a full back slam onto the ice. (Think Charlie Chaplin meets a banana peel, and you'll have the visual.) Also, I did not make that goal.

What's my point? All skating is not created equally. And not all writing is created equally. In the hands of an amateur who doesn't know the finer nuances, disaster can strike—as I proved in my first hockey experience, and as is proven in writing groups, where so many participants just don't have the depth and breadth of writing experience to offer quality critique.

Oh yes, darling, my manuscript is with my beta readers.

Ooo. Fancy. It sounds so official, makes us feel like real authors.

What can I say? I know, I know you want it, you can taste it, you can feel the embossed letters of your name on the cover of your book.

Take a deep breath. This one's going to be rough.

Beta readers are readers. READERS! *I like it. I don't like it.*

If you want that feedback, great. Send your manuscript to 80 million beta readers and throw a party. But do *not* let unqualified people muck around in your life's work and expect quality results.

How many times have I heard this: "Well, one guy said my main character should actually be a girl, but three people said he was fine as a boy, and I rewrote 200 pages, and now I'm just so confused."

Is that you?

Be honest.

What I said about your family and friends is true for 99.9999% of beta readers as well—no matter how well-intentioned they are, beta readers are still unqualified for the job.

Poor timing

Not only do you need people who have expertise in what you're writing, but you need people with expertise in *how* to give feedback.

From a neuroscientific standpoint, the timing of the feedback process is very specific.

Have the people you are trusting with your manuscript been trained in giving quality feedback? And more specifically, have they been trained in the *timing* of quality feedback?

All of the aforementioned errors are bad, but this one is the worst because getting it wrong will have long-term damaging effects on your brain. You can literally reprogram your brain into a fear mode if you continue to get feedback at that wrong time.

Have you ever met a talented writer who just gave up? Highly likely a victim of poorly-timed feedback.

That's just depressing, right? All right, let's flip the coin and talk about how to turn this thing around. Let's look at what *can* be when you get the right kind of feedback.

Hey Smarty Pants.
Line your pockets with *this*.

Download this simplified flowchart
to walk you through the steps to
find quality support to help move
you toward your writing goals.
www.writing-gym.com/support

QUALITIES OF
QUALITY FEEDBACK

WE'VE TALKED ABOUT THE consequences of getting the wrong kind of feedback and what to avoid. (At least I hope you'll avoid it from here on out!) Now, let's talk about the possibilities.

Quality feedback is based on how your brain works

Remember (like three lines ago) when I was talking about how there's perfect timing for feedback? Well, as it turns out, optimum feedback occurs in phases that match the various phases of the writing process—not the one we impress upon it, but ones which the brain actually dictates.

The key here is to use the right method at right time.

What are the neuroscientific factors behind the timing of feedback? If you don't know what these factors are, you need to find an editor and/or critique group who does. If your editor or critique group doesn't know, there's a strong possibility they're doing more harm than good.

Remember what I said above about reprogramming permanent neuropathways that lead to giving up writing?

A quality editor or critique group understands the proper time for feedback and the different types that need to be given at different times. This is not mumbo jumbo; it's optimizing your brain function so you can be best writer you can be.

· In the early stages of the writing process, your brain needs feedback that feeds creativity rather than stifles it.

If you've ever had that deflated feeling after a critique, you were likely getting the wrong kind of feedback at the wrong time.

If you're getting the right kind of feedback in this phase, the feedback process becomes a creative release that fuels you.

Can you imagine that? Feedback that *inspires* you? How often have you felt that?

Well, when you address your brain's needs, the way it works, amazing things can happen.

So many writing groups are like running a marathon backwards. Our knees are meant to bend one way, and not the other, yet so much of what we do in writing groups works against the way your brain is meant to run a marathon, if you catch my drift.

That kind of thinking might get you into the Ministry of Silly Walks, but it's probably *not* going to help you to publish your writing.

Feedback that moves the writing forward

We do not want to run a marathon backwards. We want to run forward and win—not even against all the other participants, but against our own best running time.

We've already talked about what happens when we don't receive feedback from someone with expertise in the writing field, or in our genre. In reality, it's even more complicated than that.

Not only do you want someone with expertise in your genre, you want someone who's got expertise in effectively providing critique.

You don't want to get hit with a fire hose worth of information, and you don't want to get a trickle either. You need a manageable amount, something you can work with, explained in a way you can understand and implement.

Secret Sauce: Not only do you want an editor with expertise in your genre, you want someone who's got expertise in effectively providing critique.

You need a feedback group or editor not only trained in the craft, its inner workings, but also the *synthesis* that takes place within the working parts of the narrative.

Can your editor or critique partner explain the synthesis of the narrative to you? (Do you understand what they say when they do?) *Knowing* something and knowing how to *explain* something are two completely different things.

Can your critique cronies give you the kind of quality information and feedback to move your writing forward?

There's a huge difference between saying, "The dialogue doesn't work here," and being able to articulate *what* in the dialogue doesn't work here and *how* it needs to be fixed.

The most effective feedback technique requires both knowledge *and* training in how to give feedback in a meaningful, effective way.

Are you getting this from your feedback friends right now?

Expertise in the Publishing Industry

Math question of the day:

Which is greater: the number of Stephen King's publications or the number of publishable fiction niches?

Go ahead, which one is the alligator going to eat? < > =

| the number of Stephen King's publications | _____ | the number of publishable fiction niches |

Ok, no fair. I asked you a question I don't know the answer to, but let's just say each one is a high number, and growing larger every day.

There are subgenres to the subgenres of subgenres.

Is your critiquer up to date on what kinds of short stories, novels, or subgenres publishing houses are looking for right now? Have they talked to agents, editors, and publishers recently? Do they have their finger on the pulse of the publishing industry?

If they don't, the feedback you're receiving is in a vacuum.

To continue the hockey analogy, you're working with someone who's not only *not* played in NHL, but doesn't even watch or go to games—you've got that person giving you feedback on how to play pro hockey. Hmm.

Look at this list again, and answer them for yourself, based on where you are.

- Is your critiquer up to date on what kinds of short stories, novels, or subgenres publishing houses are looking for right now?

- Have they talked to agents, editors, publishers recently?
- Do they have their finger on the pulse of the publishing industry?

More Analogies Ahead

If you answered "no" to any of those questions, you are living your writing life like the guy with a broken leg who goes to a back alley doctor to get it set with a hammer and a hanger.

Would you recommend that to a loved one?

Do you love your writing?

Why are you recommending a hack job for it?

You spent years on a manuscript, you've sacrificed vacations, family time, getting up early or staying up late.

Are you going to waste all those sacrifices by showing your work to the wrong people? To get ego feedback?

Do you want the wrong critique, partial critique ("Your dialogue is wrong."), insults on an *ad hominem* basis?

If you're depending on the free critique group for quality feedback, you may as well be going to the back alley doctor for your broken leg.

If you're going with peer-to-peer feedback only, you're doing yourself, your time, and the sacrifices you've made a terrible disservice by not getting meaningful feedback.

If you're frustrated with the feedback experience, it might be because you're going about it all wrong.

Remember that part about shifting your mindset?

It's time to look for a new kind of group.

You want a group who understands and uses the techniques for quality feedback. You want to work with trained professionals and editors who understand the feedback phases *and* understand the *how, why,* and *what* of that which needs to be improved in your manuscript.

What happens when you find the right kind of feedback?

Finding this kind of feedback for your writing can be one of the most empowering experiences of your life.

Once you find it, you'll feel more confidence in your writing than you ever have before. You'll complete more writing faster than you ever thought possible, which will lead to a finished manuscript, and you'll have the skills and confidence to publish over and over again.

You'll finally feel like, and be, the author you knew you always could be.

Part III

Craft

What do agents complain about when they think no one's listening?

In my line of work...(Did I mention I am a writing coach? I help writers become authors every day. Shameless plug, I know. But they *did* let me put my name on the cover of the book, after all.)

In my line of work, I talk to a *lot* of literary agents. When we're not talking about baseball and the stock market (just kidding; we don't talk about any of that), we talk about writers and books. I ask what they're looking for, what's trending now, and what trends they see in the submissions they're getting.

Now lean in, because I'm going to let you in on a little secret.

(Did you just lean into a book? *Silly*.)

The number one frustration I hear over and over and ov—well, you get the idea, from agents is writers not knowing their craft.

Secret Sauce:
Know your craft.

Now, you don't have to worry about being one of *those* sloppy types, because you're reading this book, and that tells me you're not only committed to learning the craft, but to submitting a quality manuscript.

You have just increased your chances of acceptance by at least 10 times.

Pat yourself on the back.

No. Really. Do it. Now.

Not only do you need to know the principles of craft, but you need to know how to apply them to your manuscript.

Well, if that's true, Annalisa, why didn't we just start with craft on page one?

Excellent question. (Have I mentioned that you are full of excellent questions?)

Here we are on page 94. That's a *lot* of pages and I haven't even gotten into the nitty gritty of craft yet?

Why?

Sloppy writing?

Lack of clarity?

Oh no, my friend. If there's one thing I am crystal clear on, it's what is *most* important to facilitating quality writing—the kind agents are looking for, the kind that's rooted in craft.

Mindset.

Working with your brain, the way it's intended to function. Writing from a place of grounded confidence. (Not some "Aw, honey" kind of lovey dovey fest, but a solid place of knowing what works, what doesn't, and where you sit.) Finding the kind of quality feedback that accelerates your writing.

Without the right mindset and support, a writing library the size of the universe isn't going to help you to become a published author.

If all we needed was knowledge, wouldn't we all get published after attending our first class or conference, or at least the hundredth?

The problem isn't "If only I knew more" for most would-be authors. It's "If only I had the confidence that would lead me to find the time to finish my book."

Are we going to dig deep into craft?

Heck ya.

Are there craft techniques that can accelerate your manuscript to publishable?

Heck ya.

But none of this craft information means *anything* if it's not built on a solid foundation of confidence, time, and support.

And that, my dear, dear writer, is why I have spent the better part of the first half of my book nurturing you into the right place to jump into technique—because that mindset is the foundation of all the work I do with writers, and the heart of my philosophy.

CHARACTER AND CONFLICT WITH A LITTLE BIT OF SETTING THROWN IN

THE PARTS OF A story are like moving gears in a machine. All the parts need to be working, and working together, for the story to move forward, but it's hard to isolate the functioning of just one.

Even though it's hard to isolate, we still need to start somewhere, because, after all, this is a book on storytelling. I'd better hop to it and talk about storytelling. Character makes sense as a starting point because:

- You can't set action into motion without someone to do it. Right, right, right. I hear you. What if we have objects do it? Well, the objects are still acting like characters. One has only to think of the dancing cartoon dishes in a certain kids' film to know how objects can act as characters. Someone or *some* thing *acting as a character* needs to do the doing.
- Some plots are character-driven, and so the character's story *is* the main story of the plot.
- Even in a plot-driven plot the character's personal struggle will dictate his or her choices, and, as a consequence, the overarching plot arc.

We'll talk more about plot types in, well, the plotting section. (I can be so logical sometimes.)

How pantsers get to know their characters

The most important thing for you to know as an author is that what *you* need to know about your characters and what your reader needs to know are two entirely separate planets.

Life is like an analogy

Photograph by by Joellen Fraizer

Here we have an photograph of a glacier, and you can see that there's only a small portion of this glacier sticking out of the water, but there's a whopper of a chunk of ice under the water.

Character is like this glacier in that you, as the author—you, as the creator of the piece—need to have this full ice and snow picture of your character. You need to know everything that's beneath the surface, *but* what you'll show in your actual story will only be that teeny, tiny piece that you see poking out above the water's surface.

So, what do I, the author, need to know, and what does my reader need to know?

I'm so glad you asked. Follow me.

In your novel, you're likely to have four-ish characters the reader will need to know in depth: certainly the protagonist, and perhaps an antagonist—and then there might be some other supporting character(s) that you'll need to know at great depth.

Of utmost importance to this Getting to Know You process is not to waste too many pages or hours trying to figure out who your characters are in the abstract—making lists of hair color, tattoos, and the brand of bike they had as a kid.

If you're a pantser (and you probably are since you picked up this book), then you are more likely to succumb to the temptation to fill an entire notebook waxing poetic on the dreams and aspirations and favorite brand of toilet paper for each character.

Look, I don't know why we do it; we just have this thing for needing to understand the setting, the plot, every quirk and motivation.

Step away from the candy bowl! You've had enough.

Ok, ok, but how do I know?

My, you *are* persistent, aren't you?

The trick here is not to get lost in listing and profiling. The most important thing you can do to get to know your characters is to see them in action. If you're not spending most of your time figuring out how your characters act or acted, you're probably wasting your time.

Consider this: You meet the perfect hottie on DreamDates-NowNowNow.com. The profile is perfect: hard-working, good-looking, down home values and even a dog (*ooo, responsible*). First date goes great, this dream date says all the right things at all the right times. Perfect. Sign me up, buy the ring, I have found *love*, baby.

Until not-so-dream-date tells off the waitress, slams the door, and has no money to help foot the bill.

Secret Sauce: If you're not spending most of your time figuring out how your characters act or acted, you're probably wasting your time.

Wait, this was so perfect. The behavior doesn't match the profile. What happened?

You didn't see Dream Boat in *action* before you made plans.

So many authors get deceived by their characters in the same way daters get let down. These are the writers who complain like chain-smoking nannies in back rooms about "misbehaving characters."

What did you expect?

You put all these expectations on them before you even *knew* them. If you just asked, if you just spent a little more time *observing their behavior*, they would have shown you everything.

So, how do we get the 411 *before* we pop the question? (If you follow my analogy; remember I *did* say life is an analogy.)

The number one thing

(This is really important, which is why I made it number one. Genius, right?)

The number one thing that you need to know about your character is what his or her goals and motivations are.

What's the main goal, and what's getting in the way? What is his or her greatest need?

Because the goal, and the struggle to get it, is what's going to drive the story, right? (We call that conflict, and we'll get to that in a bit.)

We must know: What are they seeking? What are they trying to get, and what's getting in their way?

We understand goals and the struggle to reach them as a fundamental of story; on some level we understand that the goal paradigm is the most essential element to know about a character. It might sound *really* obvious, BUT a lot of times, *especially for pantsers*, the ultimate goal isn't particularly obvious when you start out a piece. Or it might change as time goes on. You think that your main character wants to find love, but really what they wanted to find was a sense of belonging.

You can put down the tissues. No, really. There, there, it's all right.

I know. Writing is frustrating, and if we didn't love it so much we'd take up knitting or jai alai.

But since we do love writing, and we're going to keep at it, we have to accept that sometimes *it* gets to decide how it wants to get done.

For many pantsers that means that the character's motivations, goals, and ultimate journey may change completely from the beginning to the end of the process.

Secret Sauce:
In writing, as in life, it's ok to say "I don't know."

Remember that "change your perspective" thing from a few chapters ago? Well, let's try that here.

Let's see this writing journey to *discover* character motivations as a gift. So, we don't have all the answers at the beginning. That can be freeing, an opportunity to let our imaginations run wild, and get into creative flow.

We pantsers aren't totally off the hook, of course, because we'll have to do catch up work in the revision. We are never free from the obligation to know the protagonist's main goal and what's getting in their way, but the timing of that knowledge is flexible.

So, pantser: It's ok if you don't know the goals and the motivations and the needs and the

Secret Sauce:
Being a pantser who finishes and publishes a novel means being committed to repeated revision.

impediments right at the beginning, *but*—and this is really important—you need to go back in subsequent drafts until you figure it out. Being a pantser who finishes and publishes a novel means being committed to repeated revision.

We'll talk more about this later, but just know that you're going to have to go back, and go back, and go back, to make sure that everything is consistent in your novel, so you can't have a character who was seeking love at the beginning and then ends up finding a job—unless you've done some work in the middle, through revision, to explain how that goal or motivation changed for that character.

Pantsers are the kind of writers who just have to *start* somewhere and then allow themselves to be comfortable with the change that will happen. Over time, you'll know when you can let your characters misbehave a little (and drive their cigarette-puffing caretakers mad), and when it's time to step in and tell them how it's going to be.

For pantsers, a lot of the discovery happens in the writing. In other words, we must write to discover and this writing must be through setting the characters in motion.

What might this look like?

Let's jump in Arthur the Author's brain for a moment and take a listen. Shh. No, it's not illegal. This is just pretend.

So, I wrote this book because I saw on the news that someone had won the lottery but not claimed the prize, and I thought: Why would anyone do that? Were they deceased? Had they lost the ticket?

And I figured that losing the ticket was the most likely— some people are so disorganized, right? It would be easy to lose a ticket. There's a lot of tension and a lot at stake in that situation, so I decided to write about this man who loses a lottery ticket.

That's my outline: After years of playing the lottery, a man wins, but then loses the ticket.

I started with the moment he found out he'd won. He and his wife are sitting on the couch eating TV dinners on their little TV trays, watching the news. Now, Frank plays the same lottery numbers every time, so he has them memorized. His teeth nearly fall out when he sees them on the screen.

"Margie, we've won."

He stands to pull the ticket out of his wallet where he always puts it, but it's not there.

What happens next? How does his wife feel? Does he find the ticket? Well, I don't know, so I keep typing.

He reaches into all his pockets hoping it's a mistake.

"What's going on?" Margie asks.

Frank is so upset, he can't even speak. He's reaching frantically into all his pockets. How could he have misplaced it?

So I'm watching these two and I think, what makes sense? What would happen next?
"Margie, I just lost ten million dollars."

"You mean...you lost the ticket?"

"Yes, I'm so sorry."

Frank falls into Margie's arms in tears.

What's going to happen to this couple as a result of this moment? Will it split them up? Bring them together? Or something else entirely?

I don't know. I keep watching and typing.

Margie is sitting on a kitchen stool the next day; she's on the phone. "Yes, he says he lost the ticket. Well, I never liked his gambling anyway—you know that. I just don't know what I'm going to do now."

Who's she talking to? Doesn't matter. As I'm writing, I have no idea about the big picture. I'm just writing, exploring, finding what's interesting and asking questions.

Does Frank find the ticket under the seat of his car? No, that feels too easy, too cliché. Something else is going on here. Let's set them in motion again.

Margie is in her bedroom now. She's looking around as if she hopes no one sees her, which is weird because she's in her own bedroom. Why would she do that? Let's watch.

She opens the small sock drawer at the top of her dresser, rifles around like she's looking for something, and pulls out a single sock. She reaches into the sock and pulls out a folded lottery ticket that looks worn, as if it could have been in a man's wallet.

Just then, Frank walks in and sees his wife holding the ticket he's been frantically looking for for over 24 hours.

"Margie, Margie my love, you found it. We're rich. You found it."

"No, Frank, I hid it."

"What do you mean, Margie? What are you talking about?"

"Frank, I've a good mind to rip this ticket to shreds. I've told you all these years how I feel about your gambling and now you've gone and done something stupid and won."

Is she going to rip the ticket? Why does she hate gambling? What's going to happen next? I don't know.

"Sweetie. Sugar pie. Do *not* rip that ticket. It's our future. It's our..."

"Frank Doherty, don't *Sweetie Sugar Pie* me. Let me tell you right now, you can have this lottery ticket or you can have me, but it ain't going to be both."

Wow. That story changed fast and it got more interesting than just a lost lottery ticket. Which will he choose, his wife or the ticket? Why? What's at stake for him?

That's the fun of pantsing. It's like watching a movie that is taking shape right now and you get to step in and contribute. My outline was about a lost lottery ticket and what happens when a ticket gets lost. I started there, but my story roamed into something far richer and far deeper.

I just want to take a moment to highlight some of the things Arthur the Author said here and to reflect on his process.

Arthur the Author: That's my outline: After years of playing the lottery, a man wins, but then loses the ticket.

Please channel your fourth grade teacher. S/he's standing right here, right now, with the roll of gold stars, the A+s, and she's grading this outline. Does little Artie get one? No—and *GOOD!*

Notice that this accomplished author went in with an idea, a concept, and that this concept was to set the *characters in motion.*

Quick Quiz: What color hair does Margie have?

Again, Arthur the Author for the win. He doesn't waste time figuring out what his characters are wearing or whether the walls are painted or wallpapered. It's not important. And, if I can put words in the mouth of the illustrious Good Ole Arthur, I would guess he would say that if those details became important, he would fill them in later.

Arthur the Author: What's going to happen to this couple as a result of this moment? Will it split them up? Bring them together? Or something else entirely? I don't know. I keep watching and typing.

Notice how he's asking himself questions throughout the process. The characters drive a little while, then he drives, then they drive, then he drives.

He's a great turn-taker, our friend Art.

If you are a writer who complains of unruly characters, take note. Characters drive sometimes, but you're that calm driver's ed teacher who ultimately has control of the car.

Arthur the Author: My outline was about a lost lottery ticket and what happens when a ticket gets lost. I started there, but my story roamed into something far richer and far deeper.

Notice this clever move.

(I feel like I'm doing a play-by-play on SportsCenter. He dashes to the right, dribbles, pivots. He shoots, he scores.)

Arthur *does* score here, and here's why: He allowed his idea to *evolve* over the course of the writing. He came to a better idea through the writing process. He crafted a little, the characters crafted a little. He pushed, they moved. They acted, he followed. Through this give and take, the story became better (for what Arthur wanted to do) than his original concept.

A good scientist does not enter an experiment with any presuppositions. In fact, bias can ruin an experiment entirely. We writers could learn from this approach; there's power in setting action into motion, and practicing careful observation.

Pantser Peril

Sometimes pantsers can feel up to their necks in what's going on with the characters. That's peril for pantsers, or, if your prefer: the Pantser Peril. In following your character, as happened to Arthur the Author (who could be any of us, right?), you might end up in a place that you hadn't anticipated. You might end up in a place where suddenly your story changes completely.

I get it. It's scary. Maybe you don't want to feel like you're wasting time digging for gold and never finding it. One way to mitigate wasted time is through character sketches—with one caveat. Remember that I said it's better to see how your character *acts* or *acted* than to make lists of traits.

Here are some questions to help set your characters in motion.

 For Success

How did he or she meet the second and third most important character? If they met in high school, for example, that might be a very different story than if they met last week. So knowing how they met the supporting characters could be an action that will in turn be important to the action of your plot.

 *For Success*

What's the backstory of their meeting? Was there a moment that was really important when they met and will the moment they met have an impact on the plot?

 *For Success*

Likewise, how did s/he meet the antagonist? Why are they at odds? Did they get along at first, and then something happened, and now they don't get along? What happened there that this person is the antagonist in the story?

 *For Success*

How does this character get in his or her own way?
Psychologically? A physical limitation?

Recipe *For Success*

What are his or her mannerisms? Pantsers are generally visual; they often see their story playing out. So, as you watch the story unfold, observe a character's quirks. How does this person move his hands? Does she touch her hair a lot? Are they picking their nose on the subway? (Whatever, no judgments.) We just need to know: What kind of mannerisms do they have?

Recipe *For Success*

What does he or she say a lot? Does she have phrases that she is repeating? In my upcoming novel, I have a main character who repeats the phrase "thank you very much" a lot. It's kind of a sarcastic thing that she says: "I don't like that, thank you very much." This helps to identify her, and also helps to show how she grows in the story to learn to communicate better about what she needs.

How does your character talk? Does your character use their hands while talking, or not? Are there certain expressions that s/he repeats?

 *For Success*

Is his or her nationality or heritage or race a significant part of who that person is and what the tension is in the story?

Recipe *For Success*

What does his or her voice sound like? Not only is hearing a character's speech pattern an interesting way to get to know your character, but this is going to play into how your dialogue will sound, and how you will differentiate your main characters from one another.

Let's take a short jaunt down Dialogue Alley.

If you think about your friends, you might all have a similar way of speaking, in that you might all have phrases and inside jokes that you use. However, no matter how close you are, you and your best friends have different ways of speaking.

Therefore: You don't want your dialogue to be homogeneous for all of your characters. How do your characters sound different from one another?

Another activity that many writers like to use is fill out a dating profile for their characters. Now, this might be more useful for some types of characters than other types, but if you go onto any online dating site you'll see some basic questions: occupation, age, height, ethnicity perhaps, religion might be important, and just a general physical description. What does this person look like? Physicality might play into who they are.

This is just a sampling of some of the character profiling we do in the Writing Gym, but it gives you some direction on how to think about how your characters *act*.

The ultimate goal here is to get to know your characters on a deeper level, which may eventually lead you to their deepest desires, needs, and motivations.

Hey Smarty Pants.
Line your pockets with *this*.

Love these questions? Download the free worksheet to fill out for all of your characters at www.writing-gym.com/characters

Your characters must be relatable

Note that I said relatable and not likable.

Your readers don't have to like your characters, but they *must* believe them. You don't want your readers to toss the book aside with a "nobody behaves like that." (Well, unless it's a romance, but that's a slightly different scenario, right?)

Your readers have to be able to see your characters as plausible—even if the world in which they live is imaginary. If you're writing an other-worldly piece (fantasy or scifi, for example), you can have people who walk on ceilings, stand on their heads and eat through straws that pop out of their belly buttons.

None of that matters if the emotional reality of the characters rings true. When the characters' emotional reality rings true, we gullible humans will believe just about anything else you throw our way.

Let's talk about the Big HP.

We just buy the fact that Harry Potter flies around on a broom, has trees that want to wump his, well, car, and cavorts with spiders big enough to give me nightmares into next week. We accept *all* of it. Why? He's grounded in his humanity.

We feel for his mistreatment. We root for him to escape his abusive family. We dislike when others spurn him. Our empathy is engaged by Harry's situation and actions. He could jump from Earth to Saturn and back again, and we'd believe it—because we trust his emotional reality.

No matter where your story is set—in time or space—the reader must relate to how your characters behave and feel.

Quirks

Quirks are an element which lend relatability to your characters, quickly and efficiently.

Why?

We humans are just quirky lil buggers. Think of the people you work with. The guy who drinks coffee from that same Superman mug every day. (Does he even wash that thing?) Miss *I-on-*

ly-eat-organic in the lunchroom. The guy having an affair who's got to be dumb if he thinks no one hears him on the phone through the cubicle walls.

Our quirks make us annoying and endearing (depending on one's perspective), and character quirks can have the same effect.

You don't want to have too many quirks per character, but one or two really make a person relatable in his or her imperfections—the more specific, the better.

What should be specific? Why, motivation of course. (You knew I was going to say that didn't you? Have I told you how smart you are in the last few pages?)

What's the intersection of motivation and quirks?

I'm so glad you asked.

Imagine two nail-biters. What does nail biting signify?

You probably said nervousness, because that's the most prevalent connotation we have for that body language.

But consider this: If I am pensive, might I also place a nail to my lips? If I am deep in reflection, might I tap my teeth with that nail?

Sure.

Same mannerism. Two totally different interpretations.

And there's a huge difference between a nervous ninny and Rodin's muse. (Rodin sculpted *The Thinker*, in case I went too far into the depths of obscure cultural references there.)

You're going to choose a mannerism that has an impact on the plot.

A note about psychology

Before I move on, just a note about psychology. Certainly the more we can understand psychology, the more depth and the more dynamism we can give to our characters. Especially if you're writing certain types of traditional literature, getting into the psychology and the motivation of a character might, in fact, be integral to your novel.

Consider, for example, Dostoyevsky. This nineteenth century Russian novelist is a master psychologist and one of the things that he's known for is digging into the deeper motivations of his characters and being able to articulate them masterfully.

Digging deep into motivation and using person vs. self as the central conflict that carries the novel is no easy task. Yet, in *Crime and Punishment*, Dostoyevsky digs so deep into the protagonist Raskolnikov's motivation that the character's struggle with himself *becomes* the story. In fact, the reader knows little else of Raskolnikov other than how he grapples with his own internal conflict—which causes and results from the central action of the novel.

Integrating psychological elements can be an A-level endeavor, but if you want to see how a master battles person vs. self and wins, I highly recommend revisiting *Crime and Punishment.*

(Remember what I said about reading?)

How much detail should I include?

Mannerisms. Quirks. Psychology. Speech patterns...I thought you said we shouldn't include too much detail.

Secret Sauce: Every detail we include has the sole purpose of moving the plot forward.

Remember this: Every detail we include has the *sole purpose* of moving the plot forward. I don't really care that your character has short hair or long hair, unless it's helping to move the plot forward, right? If she's a fighter and she ends up getting grabbed by the hair because her hair is really long, that's important. If she always tucks it up under her helmet, we don't care about her hair.

Let's compare two scenarios and see what this looks like.

Some of you who might have met me at writers' conferences might understand that I'm, er, *vertically challenged* at a whopping five feet tall.

If I were a character in a chick lit, there might some opportunities for that to be my quirk, right? It might be comic relief that comes around about how I can never reach the cupboard. My friends, my roommates, my boyfriend, whoever in this novel is always having to get things down for me because I can never reach anything that's not on the bottom shelf.

Not only is this an entertaining attribute, but maybe as the protagonist of this novel, I am on a quest to self-acceptance, and so getting over myself and my insecurities about my height serve not only as entertainment, but as the external manifestation of my internal conflict.

Secret Sauce: Quirks can serve as the external manifestation of a character's internal conflict.

Let's genre hop, shall we? If I am the heroine of a fantasy novel, there might a different opportunity here for this quirk.

I'm short and I can never get up on my dang horse; somebody's always going to help me get up into the saddle. That's funny—but it might also be something that helps the plot to move forward. Here's one scenario: There might be this moment when it's dawn at camp and everyone's getting ready to set out on the trail. Out of nowhere, the bad guy and his crew come charging down the path toward camp.

Well, the fact that it takes me longer to get onto my horse is now a liability. Maybe I end up injured because I'm not battle-ready or perhaps I am kidnapped. Maybe my kidnapping is the inciting incident that leads my compatriots on a quest that ultimately saves the kingdom. It couldn't have happened without my quirk.

What I'm saying is consider how the attributes of your character are going to help to move the plot forward. If you're going to include a detail, such as the person being short, is that going to be comic relief only, or is that going to be something that is directly tied into conflict?

Conflict

Just so we're all on the same page, let's review the different types of conflict.

 **Person vs. person**	Well, just like it sounds, we've got a person battling a person. Luke Skywalker vs. Darth Vader. Tom vs. Jerry. Seinfeld vs. the Soup Nazi. Whatever it is that the character wants, there's another person standing in the way.
 **Person vs. self**	These are the stories about trying men's souls. (Yes, Thomas Paine just rolled in his grave. It's all good.) Sometimes we are our own worst enemy, and these stories write all about it. Whatever the character wants here, s/he's getting in his/her own way. Often what the person wants in this case is not something external (peace in the galaxy) but internal (fulfillment, love, freedom from guilt).
 **Person vs. nature**	In this conflict, nature may be literal (think Odysseus battling the whirlpool Charybdis or the doldrums) or supernatural (think Jacob wrestling with God through the night).

NB: Some people separate out "person vs. supernatural (God)" as its own category. We're not here for theological debate; this is a book about storytelling, so do what you want. They're just labels. It's more important to know *how* to use the concepts than for us to argue about what things are called.

Of course, your novel is going to have conflict. Remember at the beginning of this chapter I said that there were all these working parts of your novel? Well, we can't think about character without thinking about conflict, and we can't think about conflict without thinking about plot, and we can't think about plot without thinking about character. It's all these cogs that come together, these gears moving together that create one operating piece.

Not only will your novel have one main conflict, but—and this is what's most important character-wise about conflict—your main character is going to balance out the types of conflict throughout the story.

What?

Let's revisit our pal Odysseus. I reminded you that he dealt with a whirlpool and the lack of wind in his sails. Poor Ole Odysseus though, life was so much more complicated for him than that. He battled Poseidon, was held captive multiple times and was tempted by the sirens' song.

As you can see, Homer varied Odysseus' problems: Odysseus vs. a god; Odysseus vs. person; Odysseus vs. well, whatever the heck sirens are.

Side trip: *The Odyssey* was composed in the eighth century BC (BCE, if you prefer). We humans have been at this quality storytelling thing for a while. Think of the power of a quality story: It lasts for *thousands* of years.

The Odyssey is a long series of multiple conflicts (but very interesting, and you should definitely reread it, especially if the last time you read it was in a high school anthology). The important fictive element Homer was onto here was varying the types of conflict; that variation is what we want to aspire to in our writing as well.

Let's simplify for the sake of illustration.

Suppose we've got a knight.

If this knight gallops across the countryside, and first he fights the yellow knight, and then he fights the green knight, and then he fights the white knight, and then he fights the black knight, that's not a really interesting story. Why? Because the conflict was consistently person vs. person.

However, if we mix it up, and first our knight has to fight the green knight and then he gets caught in a storm—person vs. nature. And then God comes down from on high (person vs. supernatural—if you like) and gives him dreams through the night that cause him to suffer so much he's unsure of himself when he wakes in the morning. That's a much more interesting story.

Why?

Because we've varied the conflict types.

Vortex! Here's where the characterization comes in: Remember the quirks?

If this knight doesn't believe in God, he is going to have a very different struggle with God coming down from on high than someone who's deeply pious, right? Knowing who my character is will influence the types of conflict that he or she can face.

Then I'm going to work in all these different aspects of who this character is so that I've got different types of conflict happening throughout.

I can't vary the types of conflict until I have a deep understanding of who my character is, and who my character is is going to determine how the conflict is dealt with. (Remember the vortex? We're evolving here, moving to the next level.)

Wait, weren't we going to talk about setting?

I'm going to say something a little bit controversial about setting, something most people don't say: Treat setting in your novel as a character.

What do I mean by that?

Like details of character, details of setting can help to ground the reader in what's happening. Similar to character, you're only going to include the details that move your plot forward. Again, no matter how interesting you think that Victorian mansion is and all its ornate furniture and rooms and textures of materials over the window, we wouldn't need to know that about a character, and we don't need to know that about setting. You can also think about the ways that your setting can help to move the plot forward.

So, no gratuitous expressions of where these people are.

If you're looking for an example of setting as character that is masterfully done and moves the plot forward in a way that almost anthropomorphizes the setting itself, I strongly suggest looking at *Heart of Darkness* by Joseph Conrad, where he uses the setting as an active character, not just a passive backdrop. Again, A-level stuff.

Confused yet?

I know I've given you a lot of information, and it's hard to see, in abstract, how all these pieces fit together. (Pantser Peril strikes again.)

I understand how confusing this writing journey can be, how looking at all the moving parts individually and trying to figure out how they work together can be overwhelming. I know because I am a pantser myself—who had to discover this system to make the process work—and writers ask me these questions every day:

- What goes where?
- What should I do next?
- Do I have enough this?
- Do I need more that?

These question are frustrating because applying writing theory to the act of writing is not easy stuff. Many writers find that the right guide to help you with the integration can be the key to moving through that frustration, especially a guide who not only understands your process, but can give you targeted activities to help you muddle through the murky murky mess and get those gears running smoothly again.

WHAT IS PLOT?

IF "[S]TORY IS THE essential progression of incidents that occur to the hero in pursuit of his one goal," as David Mamet wrote, then plot is the best way to arrange the parts.

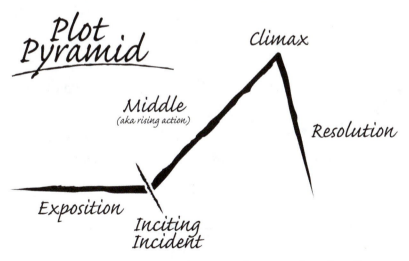

Plot Pyramid

Climax

Middle
(aka rising action)

Resolution

Exposition

Inciting Incident

When we think about the plot, we often use the plot diagram devised by the nineteenth century novelist Gustav Freytag. The plot arc covers the action of the entire novel; think of it as the rainbow over your piece, with the moving, churning water below as the tension of the individual story arcs.

We're going to use the plot diagram to discuss the elements of plot and the structure of your story—but first, let's talk about the different types of plots.

Plot-Driven vs. Character-Driven

There are two main types of plots: plot driven and character-driven.

Novels that are plot-driven focus on plot twists, action, and external conflict. Think James Bond. The goals of the story, here, are focused on external outcomes. (Will Bond catch the bad guy?) The characters make fast decisions, and therefore character development, or evolution, takes a back seat to the unfolding of events.

Secret Sauce: Novels that are plot-driven focus on plot twists, action, and external conflict.

In character-driven novels, the main focus is the evolution, or change, of a character over time. All coming-of-age novels fall under this category, and all novels in this category follow the same guidelines as a coming-of-age piece, even if they are not technically about a child coming of age. In *The Secret Life of Bees*, for example, we see a girl grow, change, and literally come of age. However, the same happens for Bridget in *Bridget Jones' Diary*, and she is certainly well above majority.

Secret Sauce: Character-driven novels focus on the evolution of a character over time.

Here's another way to think about it: In a character-driven plot, the characters seek something within themselves; the struggle may manifest itself externally, but the real journey is an internal one. In plot-driven plot, the character seeks something outside of himself: to vanquish the bad guy or to find the Holy Grail.

Re-read that paragraph again, because that's a *huge* tip.

Secret Sauce: In plot-driven plot, the character seeks something outside of himself.

Secret Sauce: In a character-driven plot, the characters seek something within themselves; the struggle may manifest itself externally, but the real journey is an internal one.

Ok, moving on.

Whether you choose to write a plot-driven or character-driven novel is up to you. Certain genres lend themselves more easily to one or the other, but these are not hard and fast rules.

You can't know which plot form to choose until you know

Secret Sauce: When considering which plot form to use, your only concern is which form will best convey your story.

your characters' motivations better, and you can't know your characters until you know what they do, and you can't know what they do until you know who they are, and you can't know who they are until...

Remember the vortex? Take a deep breath. The carousel's coming around again, and there's always a chance to grab the golden ring.

Before we move on, I want to mention that you can write a hybrid of the two forms. (I would argue that *The Hunger Games* is one such hybrid.) That said, as with anytime you create a mishmosh, you sacrifice some of the integrity of each art form. Spaghetti pizza might be yummy, but is neither spaghetti nor pizza. A hybrid novel loses some of the fast pace of the typical plot-driven novel, and lacks some of the depth and exploration of character contained in a character-driven novel. This difference is not a bad thing *per se*; it's simply something to be aware of as you choose the plot style that is going to help you to reach your end goals the best.

Going back to the idea of A-level stuff, a hybrid novel is probably a challenge that inexperienced writers shouldn't attempt yet. It is one of the "soufflés" of the writing world. That doesn't mean, like all high-level material, you can't play with it, investigate it, and explore it.

Secret Sauce:
The hybrid plot is one of the "soufflés" of the writing world.

No matter which format you choose, the plot not only includes the main goals of the story (whether they are event or character specific), but also interweaves your overarching themes, and possibly symbolism. (This is a very literary technique, and may or may not apply to your novel. In *A Tale of Two Cities*, for example, the symbols of the Golden Thread and knitting are woven throughout. Ha! Get it: woven. Are all of my jokes going to be that bad? Probably.)

What's Unique for Pantsers

As we saw in the example in the character chapter, sometimes pantsers have to write themselves into and out of plot. You may not *know* as you begin to write where your characters are going, where they begin their story, or where they end it. That's ok.

It's never too late to come back in and change things up.

Remember, this cyclical nature of writing is important to keep in mind. As pantsers, we may want the writing process to be linear, but it simply isn't. We must accept and work with the process for creative flow to happen. When we fight the process, we get in our own way, and then complain of "writer's block."

I understand. Trusting that I can come back later, that I can fix it in the revision, or the next revision, or the next, well, this can be super scary and one of the frustrations for pantsers. *What if I mess this up?*

I get it. No really, I do.

Empathy Moment Brought to You by the Letter K for Knitting

I'm a beginning knitter. I can knit a scarf with enough proficiency that it's wearable without unraveling. However, I've paused more complicated projects for years because I have messed up, I didn't know how to fix it, and I was so terrified to tear it apart, drop stitches, and start all over again. (Do you feel that way sometimes about your writing?)

So, recently when I made a mistake I didn't know how to fix, I did what any wise beginner does and I got some help.

My friend Deb is a master knitter. She takes one look at a piece and knows what needs to be done to fix it. She digs right in and starts pulling out stitches. She knows where to go and what to do. I watch her with trust...and terror.

The same is true with writing. Deb came to a place where she is comfortable tearing apart knitting, and I came to a place where I was comfortable tearing apart writing, by *doing*. You will get to that place as you grow as a writer. In the meantime, you are here to learn, just as I sit beside Deb and learn to count stitches, find dropped stitches, etc. You have made the wise decision to read this book so that you can learn and grow. That is the first step to success.

Getting the right kind of help and support is essential on your journey to publication.

The Parts of the Story

Let's get down to the business of storytelling. I am sure you know about the parts of the story. I'm going to help you to fill in some of the blanks many writing classes leave out.

Exposition

Inciting Incident

To review the parts of the plot diagram: The exposition is going to tell us the *situation normal* in your novel. What's going on before things change and chaos ensues?

Here are some of the elements you'll want to be sure to include in that section of your novel.

Characters: All the World's a Stage
Yes, the exposition is a place where you need to show us some of your main characters, but, and here's a TOP TIP: Not all of the characters in your entire novel need to appear on page one of the novel.

Imagine a play where within the first five minutes the entire cast crosses the stage and does something or other. You'd have no idea who was who, whom you should really care about, or why. In short, this would be very confusing. Such a scenario might make for a good comedy or existential satire, but if you want to put together a cohesive, understandable story, you need to introduce your characters gradually.

Introducing characters in a gradual trickle as the plot unfolds familiarizes the reader with a character's importance, and overall role in the plot.

Introducing your Setting

Another newbie mistake you want to avoid like the plague (besides clichés, I mean) is over-explaining the setting. (Remember that setting acts like a character—no gratuitous over-telling.) Your setting gets maybe a paragraph in the exposition. If you've currently written more than that, you need to seriously consider reduction.

There are, of course, exceptions—especially depending on how you use your setting as character (remember *Heart of Darkness?*)—but the days of romantic descriptions of rolling fields are over. The modern reader wants to get straight to the point; in other words to move to the inciting incident as quickly as possible.

Conflict

Lastly, your exposition introduces the main conflicts of the story. Is there a war in the background or foreground of this novel? Does the first character we meet hate the second character we meet? Is there a long family feud? Has there just been a theft? We will see these incidents right away. If your plot is character-driven, we will also see the principal character conflicts that will drive the plot.

Remember that the exposition is short. Why? Situation normal is boring! We want to start to see what's going to change and what the conflict is going to be.

Speaking of conflict, *there absolutely has to be conflict or else it's not story.* There are all kinds of interesting novels out there (especially from nineteenth century America) that are an entertaining exposé of a quaint way of life, but unless your protagonist is facing a constant conflict that he or she is attempting to overcome, you haven't got a story, you've just got a cute portrait of an age.

Be the Captain of Hooks

Your exposition begins with a hook. Your first sentence needs to make your reader want to continue reading. Furthermore, the first five pages are essential to grabbing your reader's attention (and, of course, for those of you who want to traditionally publish, the attention of both the agent and the publisher).

We talk about the seven types of hooks in the Writing Gym, but the main thing you need to remember is that a good hook follows the M rule: Mysterious and Memorable. Your hook is a mic drop kind of a statement that makes the reader want to know more, and one that won't soon be forgotten.

Need proof?

Name this novel:

> *It was the best of times, it was the worst of times, it was an age of wisdom, it was an age of foolishness, it was an epoch of belief, it was an epoch of incredulity, it was a season of Light, it was a season of Darkness, it was the spring of hope, it was the winter of despair.*

Though we may not remember the entirety of the opening sentence to Dickens' *A Tale of Two Cities*, most of us, especially in the literary world, associate "the best of times" with Dickens.

Why?

It is both mysterious and memorable.

Pattern Disrupt

Stories happen not because of situation normal (BO-RING!), but because something comes and interrupts situation normal. This "something" is the inciting incident. I like to call it the "and then." (Drawl it out like a drama queen for full effect, and you'll see what I'm getting at here.)

The "And Then" has to be big; it has to interrupt the pattern this person (your character) has been living for a long time.

- Does the character get fed up with situation normal?
- Or, in the classic hero's journey, is he called to the quest?
- Does something new come into his or her life to interrupt the pattern?

Whatever it is, we need *something* to interrupt what's been going on.

The inciting incident is the kind of thing that disrupts our lives. Consider this:

> My name is Emma and I guess I'm like most teens. Some days I hate my mom. (Who thinks yoga pants are cool? So gross.) Some days Mom's my best friend. (The day Brad dumped me to go to the prom with Loose Lips Lucy and Mom bought me the beautiful beaded dress and took me to Chez Olivier? Well, Mom wasn't so bad that day.)
>
> But lately Mom has been acting strange. (Even stranger than most moms, which is saying something.) It's not anything I can put my finger on. Well, there was the Mug Incident, when she dropped that mug in the sink and then broke into tears when it shattered. That was something.
>
> It's like she's extra nervous or something. I don't know. It's just weird and I want things to go back to normal—if you can call anything about our life normal.
>
> I am the only one in my class who not only isn't Catholic—in an all girls' Catholic school—but I'm

the only one with a single mom. As if that doesn't make me weird enough, she's a single mom by choice. I've never even met my dad—and Mom doesn't talk about it.

Whatever. We're supposed to go out to dinner tonight and I am so not into it, with the way Mom's been behaving lately. Besides, she made a reservation at Chez Olivier. It's not even a special occasion. It's a Wednesday, for Pete's sake.

I know there's no way out, so I head downstairs to get in the car. I'll just jet as early as I can and play some hoops with Beth and Charlie.

—

Dinner is an absolute nightmare.

If Mom's had the jitters for the last two weeks, tonight's an encore performance. She's dropped her fork so many times, the last time the waiter brought her a new one, he brought two. She's spilled her water glass and soaked my dress. (I can't leave at least until it dries because it looks like I've peed myself.) And she's shaking so much, the glasses keep clinking.

If I weren't enjoying the food so much, I would crawl under the table and hide. I cannot tell you how many times I have thanked my lucky stars that Chez Olivier is not the kind of place my friends frequent on a Wednesday night.

I've never been more embarrassed—and we're only on the starter salads.

"Mom, can you pass the salt," I ask. It occurs to me that she might spill all of the salt given her current condition, so I watch her hand closely.

"Hello there," A man I didn't see coming stops beside our table.

Great. I roll my eyes. That's what this was all about. Another one of Mom's flings I have to make nice with.

The man stands at the end of the table as my Mom's eyes grow to dinner plate size. She jumps to her feet, banging the table on her way up.

"God, Mom, can't you just..."

"Emma, this is your father. I, I'm sorry. We bumped into each other two weeks ago, and I just didn't know how to tell you."

"Hi," the man—my father—says, but I can't squeak out even the simplest hello.

SHOW STOPPER!

GAME CHANGER!

Emma (who's kind of a whiner, let's be honest) is about to be seriously shaken, her life will be turned upside down by the entrance of a father she's never met into her life.

That's what you want your inciting incident to be. An event that sets the course of events in a new direction.

Middle
(aka rising action)

You've heard the rumor about the middle child, right? Moody. Unpredictable. Black Sheep. All around a difficult case. Welcome to the middle of your novel.

Why is the middle so hard to write?

In the middle we ask: What events are required to get my character from here—the end of the beginning—to there—the beginning of the end? In other words, from the inciting incident to the climax, but I like thinking of those moments as the end of the beginning and the beginning of the end, as it helps to reframe them in a useful way, don't you think?

One of the reasons pantsers struggle with this section is because, well, they're pantsers. Now look, fellow pantser. Look yourself in the mirror, and repeat after me: I'm a pantser and that's ok.

You just talked to yourself in the mirror. How foolish do you feel? (Scale of 1-10. Tweet me a number @annalisaparent. Oh, this is gonna be fun.)

But seriously, folks, let me take a moment to say that one of the biggest problems we pantsers face is an identity crisis.

We want all of the answers (What happens next? What's my protagonist's motivation?)...without having to go through the treasure hunt it takes to find them.

If you're a pantser after my own heart, sometimes you want to expedite this whole process. You think, if I could only *think* my way out of this. And so you reflect, and you hem, and you haw, and your characters move nowhere. Anyway, that's what happened to me, before I found a better solution.

Your middle will not arrive through thinking. It is better to be writing, and writing something that won't make the final cut, than to be thinking about what you want to write.

Now, not to get all meta on you, but as your character muddles through his middle to save the universe or find love or whatever, well, you're on your own journey: to find your novel. (Please don't write that novel. It's got a cheese factor of Roquefort. Pee-yew.)

But if we *were* to write that story and if *you* were the protagonist in that Cheese Factory of Novels, imagine this: You're fighting your way through Pantser Palace with only a pen. That's write, er, right! Your only tool is your words. Do not be deceived by the Siren Song of Self-reflection, or "if I maybe drew a diagram" or one more plot sketch, character sketch, setting outline. NO!

You are a warrior! Fight through the despair by writing, fight through the confusion, the frustration, with *writing*.

If you understand and you're ready to write through the middle, turn the page.

If you are still clinging to your stubborn pantser ways, turn to page 19.

Ah, I see you're still with me.

Your middle, in brief, follows through on the problems presented in the exposition. So, if the two main characters hate each other, this is where they're going to become bigger enemies, or battle each other, or suddenly decide that they actually have a lot in common and they're friends.

How to Avoid the Muddle of the Middle
It's not a bad idea, especially for a first novel, to write the beginning and then the end because the middle is where many writers get bogged down in too much detail and the story gets killed.

If you know where you want your characters to end up, it can make it easier to fill in the middle because you have a North Star of sorts.

It's your job to find the method that works best for you. You can try these methods on for size.

Ground Control (to Major Who?)
One of the things that pantsers get confused about is the constant influx of new ideas, the promise of what-if. While this is exciting, it can also be disconcerting, as you'll likely feel like you're never going to finish your novel for having too many ideas. Idea swamp.

Idea swamp is where having something to ground you is essential.

There will be moments where it's useful to follow a new impulse, and others where—well, not so much.

How do you know the difference? Think back over your entire plot and ask: Will this idea serve my plot? If it's a yes or a maybe, proceed. If it's a no, invest your energy in completing your novel on the trajectory you were already traveling on.

However, even that method is not foolproof. Your character may, in fact, indicate something to you that needs to be changed.

If I've said it once, I've said it a thousand times (or at least, I probably will by the end of this book). Vortex Moment: Remember, plot creation is fluid and you, the author, need to make decisions about what is ultimately going to serve your plot and what isn't. Sometimes you won't know the end, or the beginning, or the middle or...

Part of being a novelist, and especially a pantser of a novelist, is being ok with uncertainty.

My only tip to you is that when possibility comes knock knock knocking, take a moment to look back at what has been and where the story wants to go, then decide if taking a side trip is going to be worthwhile.

Like real-life road trips, sometimes we can't see the benefit of a journey until we've done it. (Ask The Wife of Bath #ObscureCulturalReferences.)

Where do you come from? Where do you go?

Remember when I said there's no right way to write? Well, the middle is a place where that couldn't be truer. You can write the bookends, as I've suggested, or you can go with my method: pure and utter chaos.

When I am working on these preliminary stages of a novel, I do not write my chapters from beginning to end, in other words in the chronological order in which they occur. I write them as the characters reveal parts of themselves and their lives to me.

As I am doing this, of course it can get quite confusing. I often have difficulty remembering what the characters have already done, or how they met the objectives that I had placed for them (or, let's be honest, that they had placed for themselves).

Flannery O'Connor stated that stories do have a beginning, middle, and end—but not necessarily in that order.

Well, pantsers, we're off the hook!

If the beginning, middle, and end can be fluid, then so can the order in which we write them.

If you're stuck, jump forward. Or backward. Remember the fiction vortex? In the later stages of my novel writing—once I've written the bulk of the book, I sometimes feel a bit lost with all the material and what I've done so far.

Coming back to plot

One of the tools that we use in the Writing Gym to help bring some clarity to the plotting process are plot cards. These help us to identify important events and we use them in an organized system to see where we've been, what we need to fill in, and where we're going.

We identify each major scene. We evaluate what happens and how it helps to move the story forward. This last sentence that I've said is of vital importance.

Anything that does not help to move the story forward gets tossed no matter how much I like it. This is where the famous phrase Kill Your Darlings comes from.

Yes, this is tedious work, but the revision process is vital to a quality manuscript—especially for pantsers.

Hey Smarty Pants.
Line your pockets with *this*.

If you'd like to use my plot cards, you can download them at www.writing-gym.com/plotcards

Using the plot cards ensures that each and every action the character makes is directly tied to the overall plot.

I'll talk more about how I get all of the pieces to intertwine and play together in the pacing section. For now, just remember that at every moment in your novel there needs to be something at stake. If there's not something at stake, that scene gets tossed.

Climax

This is the moment in your novel where all of the story movement leads to a yes/no or either/or decision.

In a character-driven plot, your protagonist's life changed, gotten shaken up and now s/he has ended up in a spot where s/he will have to make a decision that will change his or her life forever.

In a plot-driven plot (that sounds funny, doesn't it?), there will be some turn of events that will impact all that we've been building up to. Perhaps the bad guy has captured Bond: Will Bond escape and save the day, or will he be eaten by sharks as he is slowly submerged into the tank?

The bottom line here is: one decision. The protagonist has to choose one course that precludes all others.

We're so over Zeus
Now look, the Ancient Greeks were cool and all—they threw *great* parties, the kegs, the togas.

Hmm, wait a minute. What am I talking about?

No cheating.

Many Ancient Greek playwrights used a plot technique called *Deus ex machina*; this is when God steps in to save the day.

Groan.

Why? Why do we groan when a neat solution appears from nowhere? You're reading this book about a brave hiker who gets separated from his group, survives a hail storm inside a hollowed out tree, eats grubs, tries to start a fire but can't, climbs

and climbs and climbs that mountain looking for some sign of civilization, but he can't even hear the distant hum of planes, trains, or automobiles.

Finally he finds a vantage point where he can see, and what's that? A small town about a mile away as the crow flies. He could get there before sunset. A ray of hope! At last. He turns to run down the path to salvation when a big ole bear lumbers up, licking his chops like "Man" is on the menu tonight.

Now Joe Hiker has a choice: battle the bear or jump down the steep rocky cliff. He looks back and forth: cliff, bear. Cliff, bear. The bear moves in closer and takes a swipe at Joe's shoulder. The paw is bigger than Joe's head. He'll have to jump, but, oh no, look at all those sharp rocks. Vertigo sweeps through his body, and the bear lets out a growl.

Poor Joe—how can he decide? Exit, pursued by a bear?[1]

And suddenly a helicopter swoops in...

Cheated.

Why? You invested time in caring about Joe Hiker, and you were cheated from the satisfaction of knowing his decision, of taking that journey with him. Something swooped in from outside the story as we've known it so far. You've been robbed.

Don't rob your readers. Make your protagonist make a choice.

---

[1] Can you name this obscure Shakespearean reference? #ObscureCultural-References See the FINAL COMMENTS section for the answer.

Resolution

The trick here is length. I've read books where the resolution feels trite and just one step above "And they lived happily ever after." I've read books where the author drags out the resolution on and on and on. There's no hard and fast rule, but keep in mind that you want to wrap up all or most of the questions you posed in the rising action.

Remember that not every plot line needs to have a happy ending, or needs to be tied up neatly. It's ok to have some ambiguity. After all, that is the realistic situation we all live in. Modern literature (Twentieth century and beyond) began by picking up some of the ambiguity of the human condition and, as time went on, began to revel in it and even make its absurdity and abstraction a centerpiece.

In a world where moral absolutes seemed evasive, ambiguity became the order of the day.

It's up to you how tightly you want to tie your loose ends, and how much you want to leave up to the reader's imagination.

Also, consider this: if you are thinking of a sequel, the resolution's a really good place to leave a few loose ends to pick up in the next book.

WHAT IS PACING?

IF PLOT IS THE *order* of events, pacing is the *rate* of the events; it's how you maintain tension.

When I was a kid, my brother and I thought the song "There's a Hole In the Bucket" by Harry Belafonte was *hilarious*.

Henry's got a hole in his bucket and he doesn't know how to fix it, so he asks his wife, Liza, for a solution. She suggests a stick.

Poor Henry. He's having a bad day!

> The stick is too long (problem)
>
> > Cut it (solution)
>
> With what shall I cut it? (problem)
>
> > An ax (solution)
>
> The ax is dull (problem)
>
> > Sharpen it (solution)

The song goes on and on like this in a pattern of problem/solution. This structure is a good example, in a microcosm, of the tension relationship that should be happening in your rising action. Will Henry ever fix the bucket? Let's keep turning pages and see. What makes us turn pages? There's a new problem.

Not only do we turn pages, but the tension here is both balanced and economical. For every problem, there's a solution, and no problem or solution is extended longer than the others.

We're going to talk about those attributes in detail in this section, but first, let's talk about the relationship between pacing and the revision process.

As I mentioned before, for pantsers, the writing is in the revision. I would *further* argue that the revision *is in* the pacing.

Before we can address pacing and do it justice, we need to know if we're ready to revise.

Secret Sauce:
The writing is in the revision and the revision is in the pacing.

How do you know when you're ready for revision? Read on, my friend.

Are we there yet?

Writers ask me all the time, "How do I know when my book is done?" Well, it's never *done*, but you can sense when it's *complete*: when all the characters arcs are tidy, and the plot arc comes round. There's no science to this one; it's just an overall feeling of wholeness to your piece.

When you're at that point, you've filled in as many blanks as you can see, you're ready for revision.

Can you think about pacing in the prewriting and writing stages? Sure, but it is a far more useful consideration in the revision stage.

Something I've never seen any other writing book or course do is address *when* in the writing process to start thinking about each of these elements.

That's the hard part, right? Figuring out *when* to do *what*.

This chapter is going to help you to start thinking about that process.

To that end, this Secret Sauce is a big hint!

Here's another hint: The most important element to keep in mind as you are working through the revision is the reader's experience.

Secret Sauce:
Polishing your pacing
happens in the revision.

A writer once told me that the worst writing advice he'd ever gotten was to write for the reader. Shouldn't you write for yourself? he asked. Once again, we have a case of a guru giving advice without telling the recipient *how* to use it. (Are you as frustrated as I am with that kind of feedback?)

Yes, you should write for yourself. *And* you should write for your audience. What do I mean? Remember the creative phases we talked about in the brain? The question of for whom you are writing functions in much the same way. The first draft, when you are just getting the story out (Ok, we all know it usually takes more than one draft), is 100% self-indulgent bubble-bath luxury. It is all about you, the author, playing, exploring and enjoying yourself.

But in the revision phase (remember we were talking about revision?), you keep your eye on your reader.

So, if the three most important things to keep in mind when buying a house are: location, location, location; then the three most important components of revision and pacing are: audience, audience, audience.

Secret Sauce:
The three most important components of revision and pacing are: audience, audience, audience.

There are two main components to quality pacing: balance and economy.

Balance and economy are similar in that they both consider the quantity of any given element you add, refocus, eliminate, or change altogether.

Let's step back into the kitchen. Everything in a recipe works in relationship to everything else, right?

So, "How much pasta do I need?" is going to depend on the flavor I am going for. Two pieces of pasta for a whole can of sauce wouldn't work very well. There has to be a balance.

Let's explore: Some people put sugar in their spaghetti sauce, and a little goes a long way! Using just a little is *economy*, but the ingredient (sugar, in this case) is still acting in proportion to the other ingredients—one teaspoon may be underwhelming in a pot to feed an army, and overwhelming in a single serving.

Similarly, the elements of quality writing are always working in balance with one another (Balance) and in reasonable proportions to one another (Economy).

THE SECRET TO THE SAUCE

Balance i.e. How much pasta do I need to balance out the sauce?

Economy i.e. How much is too much/too little based on how much of the other ingredients I have?

I've broken the pacing sections into two subsections (balance and economy), but keep in mind that, like all of the other elements we've talked about, in *practice* they are intertwined.

Let's step into the kitchen again. Scratch that. Even better, let's step into the dining room.

We're sitting down for pasta night and I hand you a hot, steaming, delicious breadstick, just the right amount of melted Parmesan and sea salt. Before you take a bite, do you want to chat about the amazing attributes of yeast and flour?

Probably not.

Your mouth is watering because of the effectiveness of the *interrelationship* of the ingredients. The attributes of each one are irrelevant—when they work together *well*. When they don't, we all know, whether we're talking breadsticks or novels, right? We feel when something is out of balance, there's too much of something, not enough of something else.

This effective intertwined, well-crafted mess is what you're shooting for and what we're going to talk about: how these two ingredients work *together* to create a quality reader experience—a third entity greater than the sum of its parts.

Please pass the Gestalt.

BALANCE

Stake and a side of fries

AH, THE PARIS BISTROS and their quintessential *steak frites*. Imagine people-watching, gathering information about human behavior—our quirks, our gestures—not far from the *Palais Chaillot*. You jot notes in your leather-bound notebook and sip your miniature cup of *espresso*.

But I digress, and all for the sake of a cute title.

The *real* point here is that there must always be steak, er, *stake* in your writing.

Secret Sauce:
At every moment—every scene, every chapter, every *word*—there must be something at stake in your novel.

Always having something at stake is the underlying principle behind each of the points I am going to guide you through in this section.

The great novelist Henry James wrote in *The Art of Fiction*: "What is character, but the determination of incident? What is incident but illustration of character?"

As you can see in the diagram above, these two elements push one another forward through the novel.

Notice that we have here another vortex, a cyclical pattern with increasing strength. What's at stake for the character pushes the incident. What happens moves the character. And around and around we go. Not only is a vortex the nature of novel writing, but of the novel itself. (Whoa, *meta!*)

I Gots to Use It

Once upon a time, I was a Kindergarten teacher with the Teach for America program in the Mississippi Delta. My students used a colloquialism I found both charming and endearing. Rather than ask, "May I go to the bathroom?" they would say, "I gots to use it," usually accompanied by a pee dance.

Here's how you're going to *use* this gratuitous anecdote: You've got to create a sense of urgency in your writing. You've got to go *now*. We need an answer *now*.

Secret Sauce: Every moment in your novel needs to carry a sense of urgency.

Remember there's a balance, but even over breakfast, there needs to be something at stake. Don't waste a single moment of your novel.

Urgency and stakes are two sides of the same coin.

- Stakes are what the author creates.
- Urgency is what the reader feels.

Use whichever perspective helps you to create a page-turner. (We'll talk in depth later about how to do that, but every quality novel needs to have a heavy dose of one of these main ingredients.)

Let me play with urgency for a moment. (Indulge me. Remember what I said about the importance of play to creativity.)

> *I can't take it anymore,* she thought as she fumbled with the house keys. *That damn door.*

It was another thing she'd asked David to fix, one of things he'd "get around to."

"I'll get around to it, honey." How many times had she heard that as the spoon clinked in the glass, stirring round and round? Chocolate milk. Cinnamon milk. Cinnamon *blueberry* milk.

It was an obsession.

She jiggled the key and finally found the sweet spot.

If he puts that milk jug back in the refrigerator one more time *without the lid, I will walk out without a word.*

The door swung open on the third push, and Doris nearly dropped the heavy grocery bags hanging from her wrist.

She fumbled her way across the living room toward the kitchen to the now too familiar dirge: *Clink. Clink. Clink.*

"Hi hon." David looked up at her from the open fridge, his arm extended into the white light.

Doris bit her lip as she heard the familiar thud of the heavy jug hit the shelf.

She closed her eyes, unsure how long she could carry the heavy load.

He shut the refrigerator door and turned to her.

"Have a good day?" David asked as he lifted the glass of milk to his lips.

You want to know, don't you? Is there going to be a milk cap on the counter when she gets to the kitchen? Is she going to leave him? Look, I just made you care about a milk cap.

Now this is just an exercise in silliness, and this story isn't really going anywhere, but the point is: Use urgency, create and maintain tension in every object (doors, grocery bags, and, yes, milk caps), every gesture, every thought or word spoken.

Try it. Let me know how it goes.

REMEMBER THAT LIFE'S A GREAT BALANCING ACT
—DR. SEUSS

There's a lot to balance in life, and there's a lot to balance in fiction.

What to balance in fiction

In fiction we need to balance emotional intensity, action, and character complexity.

What you need to balance and *how* you need to balance them will depend largely on what type of plot you are working with.

As we saw in the plotting chapter, both plot-driven and character-driven plots have elements of action and emotional depth, but plot-driven novels focus more intensely on action than character development, and character-driven novels do the converse.

This fact is going to influence what needs to be balanced in any given novel.

If you're working on a character-driven novel, you'll need to balance the emotional intensity of the overall piece.

If you're working on a plot-driven novel, you'll need to balance the pacing of the action.

Remember: There are no hard and fast rules here. Every novel contains elements of action *and* character development. Balance is always essential. What I mean is: Don't skip ahead to the next section. (I knew what you were up to.) Just because you write plot-driven novels doesn't mean you don't need to understand the importance of balancing emotional intensity, and vice-versa.

Emotional Intensity

One of your jobs as a writer is to evoke emotion. Ever cried at a movie? Quality writing.

(Personally, as a child, I excused myself to the bathroom at the end of *The Sound of Music* Every. Single. Time. so no one would see me tearing up. I don't think I've ever told anyone that. My secret's safe with you, right?)

Evoking emotion is a great responsibility. Consider these two friends.

1) The Drama Queen. Everything's urgent. Everything's a disaster. Everything's certain death and no solution.
2) Mr. Understatement. He's the guy who breaks his back, hobbles himself to the hospital, then mentions it nonchalantly six months later. He's Mr. Buttoned Up. My lips are sealed. I-got-nothin' Dude.

Ok, so maybe you've got these people in your life, and a whole bunch of normal friends. (Is there such a thing as normal friends?) It's an average Saturday night, you want to hang out, whom do you call?

Normal friends. Almost every time. Right?

Why? We like to limit our emotional extremes, in general. Sure, we hang out with the others *sometimes*. We like them; they may even entertain us. (They *definitely* entertain us.) But they can be exhausting.

Spending time in emotional extremes demands energy from us. It's ok from time to time, but we don't, typically, make it a lifestyle. We are, for the most part, programmed to avoid living in emotional extremes. (Remember the brain and its stress response?)

And yet...

The rules of writing are nothing like the rules of real life.

In real life we censor ourselves, leave out the gory or embarrassing or overly personal details of the stories we tell about our daily lives.

In writing, we have to be so brutally honest about the human emotional reality of the situations we portray, we are left feeling exposed—if we have done our job right.

Good writing is—unlike all of the people with which we are surrounded—and even ourselves, if we dared be totally truthful about it—honest to the point of purity.

Perhaps this is why those of us who love to read have such a deep connection to quality writing: Its honesty is such a relief, so compelling, such a breath of fresh air, that we miss the characters-turned-friends once we've come to the end of a good yarn.

Good writing is that guy you invariably end up sitting next to on the plane who wants to tell you every detailed encounter with the junior high bully, or every hobby his grandkids ever pursued...except when it's *good* writing, it's actually *interesting*. The story is compelling even though you're not male or have never crossed paths with your school's bully or have no kids nevermind grandkids. It has an emotional reality to it so convincing that not only do you believe it, you *feel* it—and you want more.

This is what good storytellers do. Yet doing so is surprisingly difficult, which is perhaps why Hemingway compared writing to sitting in front of a typewriter and bleeding. If we're doing it right, the rawness of our humanity bleeds out onto the paper.

The process to create writing that is true to the human experience is akin to the Velveteen Rabbit's process of becoming real. "Does it hurt?" the rabbit asks in Williams' children's story.

Where writing is concerned, yes, it hurts. It hurts because it is difficult to draw on those emotional reserves, to extract the essence of the most challenging moments we have lived through, and because honesty—especially with ourselves—can be unnerving even in small doses.

But is it necessary? Absolutely. Writing that is inauthentic is writing that is forgotten and put down.

Secret Sauce: Writing that is inauthentic is writing that is forgotten and put down.

When we write, we are given permission to break free from the mold of societal expectations about oversharing. In fact, our stories fall flat due to *under*sharing.

And like the Velveteen Rabbit's becoming real, learning to share at this level, to reach those depths of honesty with ourselves and our readers, and finding the voice to express it, all take time.

> 'It doesn't happen all at once,' said the Skin Horse. 'You become. It takes a long time. That's why it doesn't happen often to people who break easily, or have sharp edges, or who have to be carefully kept. Generally, by the time you are Real, most of your hair has been loved off, and your eyes drop out and you get loose in the joints and very shabby. But these things don't matter at all, because once you are Real you can't be ugly, except to people who don't understand. (Williams)

The same could be said, I would argue, for the creation of good writers.

Writers must be real—first with themselves and, in turn, with their audiences. We must be willing to be the oversharer on the plane to the point of hyperbole, to tell not only the story, but to reveal its deepest emotional and psychological underpinnings. This catharsis requires a lot of mining. (The process may also be why Hemingway suggested writing while intoxicated, but that's a different topic for another day.)

So, go ahead: Put yourself out there. Be "that guy" on the train. Be the grandma with the wallet-sized photos of her plethora of grandchildren. But tell it *real*. Tell it *raw*. Be, as a writer, the person polite society rejects in walnut-panelled parlors for saying what was best left unsaid.

Oversharing is the burden of being a good writer, but it is, too, its simultaneous freedom.

Make Up Your Mind!

"Ok, so what you're telling me, Annalisa, is that I should not be too emotional, but I've got to be super emotional. Which is it?"

Yes.

The trick to quality writing is to be *real* without being *dramatic*.

This is what people mean when they say, "Avoid sentimentality."

Secret Sauce:
The trick to quality writing is to be *real* without being *dramatic*.

Because we are programmed to limit emotional stress, you, as the writer—as the emotional mitigator of the novel—have an important job to do.

You need to balance the emotional swings of your novel.

|- - - - - - - - - - -|- - - - - - - - - - -|
Eeyore   Pooh   Tigger

Let's step into the Hundred Acre Wood. You've got Pooh, and Tigger, and Eeyore. Who gets the most time center stage? Pooh. Why? He's neutral. Tigger, like, ohmigosh and what, and now I'm here, and oop, here we go, and woohoo. I love Tigger, but he takes a lot of energy to hang out with.

And then there's Eeyore. Oh Eeyore, so sad and dreary, down in the dumps Eeyore. Sad, sad Eeyore. That takes a lot of energy too, right?

You are swinging the pendulum between these two ends *and*: To every action there is also an opposite and equal reaction. (That should be, like, a law or a rule or something.)

Secret Sauce:
In writing (as in physics) To every action there is also an opposite and equal reaction.

Most of the emotional tension is going to take place right around the middle (Pooh), but if you swing to high, sometime soon you've got to swing the same distance toward low.

How do I know which is which? How do I measure?

Again, another frustrating element of writing and revision, because there's no unique answer. The godsend here is that

we, as writers, like actors, in general, have an entrenched sense of empathy. We can usually *feel* what is right once we read through a draft.

Secret Sauce:
We writers have an entrenched sense of empathy. We can usually *feel* what is right once we read through a draft.

AND...ACTION!

In real life, we have lots of goals, dreams, and aspirations. We've got several projects that take up our time: our family, friends, home, jobs, etc.

Characters are not afforded this luxury. While you don't want your characters to be flat or one-dimensional, they are *limited*.

What am I talking about? We are complicated, we human beings, with a constant internal monologue and conflicting desires and, and, and. This complexity is

Secret Sauce:
While you don't want your characters to be flat or one-dimensional, they are *limited*.

not only difficult to convey, but it's difficult for the reader to keep tabs on.

If the readers knew the characters on the same deep level as they know those who are closest to them, _and_ (and the "and" here is important) they followed along on their adventure and knew all of the details, that would be overwhelming. There would be too many threads to keep track of. As the author, you choose which threads to go deep on, and which to only scratch the surface with.

Remember that thingie I said about balance. Here's another balancing act.

So, if you're writing a psychological novel, and you're digging deep into character, you're probably going to have fewer characters and less action. If you're writing a quest, you'll likely have a lot of action and perilous situations, and maybe one character we know well, but not too, too well.

Case in point: Detectives in crime fiction novels are working to solve only one mystery. In reality, of course, detectives work several cases at once.

Why is the balance of limitations important? Can you imagine the scenario where we have a detective working on the blue case and discovering the body, then running off to the red case where the fingerprints have just revealed the identity of the murderer, Colonel Mustard, and now he's got to dash off to the conservatory to reinvestigate the crime scene. But wait, there's a phone call about the blue case...

I am exhausted just thinking about it.

One of the conventions of this genre is to simplify narrative by handling one case at a time. (In general. All rules, of course, have exceptions.)

Consider how you need to *limit* some plot elements in order to *enhance* others in your narrative.

(There's that thingie about balancing again.)

Secret Sauce: Consider how you need to *limit* some things, in order to *enhance* others in your narrative.

The point here is balance in your reader experience. Remember at the beginning of this chapter I told you the three most important considerations in pacing: audience, audience, audience? Well, here's how you take heed of that advice.

Hey Smarty Pants.
Line your pockets with *this*.

Download this free table to help verify that all of your plot points are serving to move your plot forward.
www.writing-gym.com/economy

If you make your plot non-stop exciting with a bad guy around every corner, it's going to exhaust your reader. Likewise, if you lumber to your point and beat around the bush, your reader is going to get tired and put down your book.

You will have high-excitement moments. You will have emotionally difficult moments. And the bulk of your novel will be just regular old getting from here to there moments: entertaining, lots at stake, but not overly emotionally charged.

On Being a Character

Sometimes English-teacher types (We won't mention any names; save that for your therapist.) like to throw around lots of fancy lexicon without telling you *why* it matters.

"Hamlet is a dynamic character whose character arc is juxtaposed by...blah, blah, blah..."

You've tuned out. They're showing off, and you're not interested.

I know. I was never that teacher. (God help me; I *hope* I wasn't!) And I am not that writing coach, so here's, uh, what we goin' ta do.

Let's review character types, and I'm going to tell you *why you should care.*

Wait, characters? Wasn't that a few chapters ago?

Uh huh. I knew you were smart. That's why I like you. Keep reading.

We have two main ways we talk about characters. They are either dynamic or static AND either round or flat.

Let's talk about science again.

Stop rolling your eyes.

In physics, that which is dynamic is that which is related to force of motion. Motion. Keep that word in mind.

Again, in physics, that which is static is that which does *not* produce motion.

Ok, science lesson over. You may wipe the sweat off your brow now.

Look, I don't *know* why we writers borrowed terms from physics, but we did. Here's how the terms apply: Characters who are dynamic *move*, they go somewhere, they change. They used to be sad, now they're happy. They were searching for a job, now they have a fulfilling career. They used to be lonely, now they're dead.

That got dismal fast.

A character who changes over the course of the story	A character who stays the same throughout the story

Moving on.

When we think about flat vs. round characters, we're thinking about how well we know the characters.

A round character is someone we know well, they're fleshed out, if you will. They're in 3D. A flat character is someone we know very little about, and don't need to. These are movers and shakers in the background of the story.

For all y'all visual learners out there, here's the skinny:

Flat

Round

vs.

A character we have limited information about

Usually background characters

A character we know a lot about

Think mirror, mirror on the wall

Ok, vocabulary lesson over.

Some of those English-y types also think they're teaching you important concepts, when really they're just teaching you what words mean. I claimed not to be one of those hooligans, so let me prove it.

Let me tell you *why you care* about these words, and why this aspect of character belongs in the pacing section.

When you consider your characters, you'll want to make sure that you have appropriate *balance* of character types. This is not nineteenth century British literature; we do not need every character fully fleshed out. (No offense to some of my favorite authors: Austen; Dickens; Thackeray...)

Think of a see-saw when you balance this section. If you've got one round character, be sure to have a flat one to balance him out; same goes for static and dynamic.

Were you the kid who tried to move in front of the see-saw seat, tried to move down the pipe, closer and closer to the middle to see if you and your friend could balance exactly evenly and hover in the air?

Good! Be that author. Balance out the *degree* to which your characters are flat and round, dynamic and static.

The key to a good novel is to have every aspect in balance.

Yes, this is why writing is work.

Think of your favorite sitcom.

- Every moment of intensity is balanced with a moment of down time.
- In each episode, a different character faces some challenge, while someone else fades into the background.
- In the middle of the battle, Lancelot is not *also* having an existential crisis. He's just slaying the dragon (or whatever).

And now for...

The Rainbow Bridge from Balance to Economy

We'll be back, after this chapter break.

ECONOMY

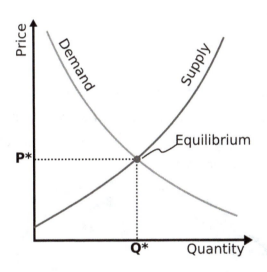

WHEN IT COMES TO the economy, what you've got to understand is the relationship between supply and demand. The price of any commodity is determined by the relationship between its supply and its demand. Whenever there is a surplus of a good...

Uh, wait. Wrong book.

When we talk about economy in *writing*, what we're really talking about is being economical. We often equate economical with penny-pinching, and to be sure that is one means of economy. When we use the term in writing, however, we mean: the opposite of being profligate or wasteful.

You are *not* the prodigal son here. You're the son who stayed home.

(I'll take Biblical References for $2000, Alex.)

In other words, don't be wasteful.

Great, got it. What aren't we wasting again?

When one is economical in writing, one uses one's space wisely, like in a poem, or as if this is your last piece of paper and bit of ink to get your message out into the world. An economical writer is one who does not overuse words, who does not use two words when one will do.

Secret Sauce:
Use as few words as possible to convey your idea.

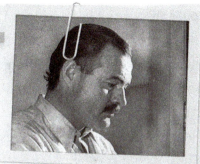

Let's take a look at Hemingway for a moment. Here is an author who is known for his brevity. He never uses two words when one will do. He could be the poster child of economy.

How did he learn this important skill?

Journalism.

Before he was a famous author, Hemingway was a reporter at The Kansas City Star.

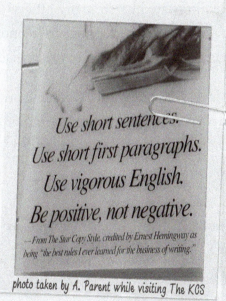

Use short sentences.
Use short first paragraphs.
Use vigorous English.
Be positive, not negative.

—From The Star Copy Style, credited by Ernest Hemingway as being "the best rules I ever learned for the business of writing."

photo taken by A. Parent while visiting The KCS

Back in the days before digital news, print newspapers only had so much space—they were limited by the size of the paper, see?

Journalists write in a special form called the inverted pyramid; this form ranks information by importance, placing what is most important at the beginning of an article, and least important last. Part of the reason for this organization is reader interest. (Most newspaper readers don't read the full article.) However, it's also in the interest of space. Back in the day the editor would start chopping off from the bottom up. This system meant that the most essential information would always be printed.

Hemingway, like so many others who had newspapers as a training ground, learned to economize. There was only so much space; he needed to use it wisely.

Today, with our word processing programs and online articles, these considerations are less important. For the most part, we can take as much room as we need—and so writers

FILL THE SPACE.

The art of being concise has been lost in many ways due to these new publishing media, and this shift has led to an increase in sloppy writing.

Sloppy writing loses clarity and your message gets lost in too many words.

Don't want to be a Sloppy Joe?

Write as if you've got limited space, and see how your writing improves.

On Being a Character

Wait, didn't we already see that section?

I told you you were smart. Stick with me as we talk about...

...The Rainbow Bridge from Balance to Economy (part two)

In the previous section we talked about the importance of *balance* in character types. Closely related: what elements the plot needs to move it forward. This is where *economy* comes in.

Remember the glacier?

As authors, we need to know the whole life story of our characters; we need to understand why they do what they do, who they are, where they came from, and where

Secret Sauce: When it comes to characters, we only tell the backstory that moves the plot forward.

they're headed. But in the revision, when we're considering pacing, we only include what moves the plot forward.

Considering economy in the revision of character arcs means considering what's included and what's not. Now is the the moment we figure out what goes above and below the water's surface. (You're still following the glacier analogy, right?)

Remember way back in the Introduction when the circling little string pen was at your feet to demonstrate the evolution over time of the creation of a novel?

Well, the string's at your waist now. *Now* is the moment in the vortex where you're ready to make more advanced decisions. You couldn't make those decisions when the string was at your feet because you didn't have enough material, enough information about character motivation to work with.

The work of what's included and what's not is the main work of revision, which for pantsers is all about polishing the pacing. Which, in turn, is why this aspect of character belongs in the pacing section, not the character section.

Aaaaah. Vortex. Here's a little something for you visual learners:

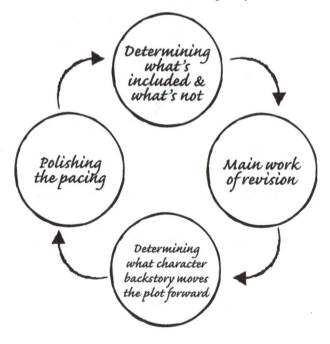

Remember when I promised you I would tell you *why* you care? Well, I just did.

Being economical with your time

When you're drafting a character, you might know whether she is flat or round. Being a pantser, though, you already know that anything and everything may change in the drafting—including who's round and who's flat.

No sense hiring a bathroom remodel in the Pantone color of the year, only to discover you hate it and you're out $20K. *What?*

In other words, don't get too attached to an idea before you've fully explored it. There are aspects of character which are great to consider *once you know the characters* very, very well, once you've set them in motion and seen what they do, where they go. Waiting to consider some of these aspects until the revision stage can help you to avoid getting lost in the rabbit hole of sitting around thinking about the characters and making them fit somewhere.

Many a writer has gotten lost in the trap of *thinking* about writing in the drafting stages rather than writing in an order, with a method, that will allow the answers to those questions unfold when they need to.

What Makes a Page Turner?

REMEMBER: The reader turns pages, and continues to turn pages, in the interest of answering a question.

What kind of question?

Details about setting? No.

Character appearance? No.

We can use these *symbolically* to move the plot forward, but no one cares about the fabric on the sofa *unless* it serves a purpose. (Red is boring. Blood-stained is intriguing.)

The kind of questions we're talking about here are about the central desires of your characters and of the plot.

Economy means that every single word should serve the purpose of answering a question. There is one (sort of) exception to this rule. I'm going to tell you about the exception, and then I am going to tell you why the exception isn't an exception at all.

The envelope, please. And the exception is...comedy.

ENTER Professor Parent [STAGE RIGHT]

Comedy can be used well and effectively to break up the tension in your piece, to give your reader a break, as it were.

Shakespeare was on to this trick, and all of his tragedies contain comic moments. (Notice I said tragedies there. Yes, all of his *tragedies* include comedy. Isn't that inconsistent? Read on.)

Let's consider Hamlet. The Prince has gone mad, and has been sent to England. Upon his return to Denmark, he finds a grave digger digging a grave. (What else would he be doing?)

Word play and avoiding the question in a "who's on first" fashion ensues.

(I have a strong preference for the BBC's 2009 adaptation starring David Tennant. If you're looking to revisit this classic, which I strongly recommend, I advise checking out this version.)

This scene does *a lot*, but for the sake of economy, I'm going to focus on three major roles this scene plays in the larger context of the play.

> LAERTES (Aside) Me thinkest there may have been some punny type insider jokes in that sentence.

First, the scene provides comic relief for the reader. Why does Shakespeare bother with comedy here? In other words: Why is the inclusion even worth noting? Balance. At this point in the play, we've just come from some really heavy material, and we're about to launch into a sharp spike that will lead to the climax. This comic scene acts like a buffer between two emotionally intense parts of the play.

Shakespeare has in mind the reader experience, and gives the reader a break before getting even more intense than the play has been up until this point. It's a clever little nest to prepare the reader, like a calm before the storm. He has balanced emotional intensity with a little pit stop at the Comedy Club.

Secondly, in Yorick (one of the dead guys whose skull is tossed from the grave during the digging), we have a symbol that serves the overall themes of the play. Yorick is the court jester on whose back Hamlet rode as a child.

In this moment, Hamlet comes to terms with the ephemeral nature of life. Hamlet looks at this skull and reflects on the lips he used to kiss, lips that are no longer there.

This realization helps him to come to terms with the question he's been grappling with for the entire play. (No, not "to be or not to be," silly: whether or not to kill his uncle to avenge his father's death.)

Here we have an excellent example of economy: Shakespeare uses Hamlet's confrontation with a skull not only as comic relief to balance emotional intensity, *but* he also uses it as a turning point in the action, small though it may be.

Shakespeare has killed two partridges with one pebble (or something like that) in this moment, by having this one scene serve multiple purposes. That concept lies at the heart of economy.

But wait, there's more.

Why does Shakespeare have staying power? Because we are deeply in love with Middle English? No. Because his stories, though over 500 years old, still strike a chord in what it means to be human. They ring with authenticity. (Remember when we talked about the power of relatability?)

Want proof? By having the jester serve as the catalyst for the climax of the play—the murder, the main tragedy—he hints at the enigmatic intertwining of comedy and tragedy. Who cares? Isn't this all English Professor-y mumbo jumbo?

Not really. Shakespeare has gotten to the essential nature of what it is to be human. Have you ever seen someone laugh at a funeral? Or cry while laughing? This quandary, this seeming disparity, is at the core of the human experience, and by digging into it, Shakespeare has made the reader feel some of the ambiguous angst that has plagued Hamlet throughout the play.

This is A+++ level stuff from a writing standpoint. (Obviously, it's Shakespeare.) But it's a standard to aspire to as writers, to try on, and work through.

Every scene, every moment, every word should help to move *something* along: theme, plot, character arc—and if you can kill two or more roadrunners with one rock? Bonus points. That's when the exception isn't an exception at all.

Economy in the exposition

Ok, so we all want to be the next Shakespeare, and we're probably not going to get there (at least I'm not), but here are a few tips you can try to get yourself a little closer to touching the threads on the hem of the robe of greatness.

Pacing is important throughout your novel, but if I had to choose a time when it's most important, I would say the exposition.

The exposition is an area where many beginning writers fall flat. Why?

It's usually because these writers wait too long to give us the problem. The temptation for beginning writers is to give too much backstory in the exposition. You want to tell us how the two best friends met and what color hair they have and the description of the bench that they're sitting on in the park in the city. You get the idea.

Remember the secret sauce about backstory? No? Ok, I'll tell you again. (You could take notes, you know.) You, the author, need to know your characters' entire histories. You need to know your characters as well as, or better than, your best friends. But at the end of the day, there is very little that you need to share with your reader.

Secret Sauce: If the detail doesn't help to move the story along, don't include it.

Finding this balance is one of the main challenges of pacing. Yes, we need to understand your characters. No, we don't need an entire FBI file on them.

The same goes for setting and any kind of physical description. We need to know we're in the woods. We probably don't need the lowdown on tree bark.

Hey Smarty Pants.
Line your pockets with *this*.

Hear more writing earworms in this video *From Mire to Page-Turning Momentum: Three Plotting Mistakes that Keep Writers in the Slush Pile.* www.writing-gym.com/balance

The problem for us pantsers is that, for the most part, we're not going to know what helps to move the story along until we're able to see the story. And we can't see the story until we've finished at least one draft. (If you're anything like me, it might take you several drafts to decide on the final plot arc.)

You can't make detail decisions until you've completed the final plot arc.

Again, that is why I say that pacing happens in the revision phase, and in the revision phase, you need to go *back* to the exposition and start pulling weeds, now that you know where your story's going.

Here's an example. A beginning writer might be tempted to start a story off telling us how a couple met, how they fell in love, and how their relationship eventually went sour when one of them committed some egregious error. (Leaving underwear on the floor perhaps?) We might get a lead up to who's at fault, with multiple perspectives on how the characters got to where they are now.

Why is it tempting for beginning writers to start a novel this way? Easy. That's how we, as writers, start a story. When we first meet our characters and begin to get to know them, we see their origins, their physicality. Like meeting a new person, we start to get to know them slowly over time.

However—and this is very important—you're not going to write your characters' story in real time. Your job as an author is to be a *storyteller*. Storytellers are engaging. Storytellers mesmerize us. Storytellers could keep you enthralled for an hour telling you about some guy who couldn't open the mayonnaise jar.

Here's a moment where a *storyteller* might start the story:

> "I want a divorce," David said. He flicked the signal to turn into our drive, like any other Sunday afternoon.
>
> "What?" I asked. I ran my hands over the soft, blue silk of my best church dress.
>
> I tried to focus on his words as he put the car in park, but all I could think of was the trunk full of groceries, and that the ice cream must be melting by now.

Now, I just wrote that on the fly. Nobody's calling me on the phone offering me prize money and round trip tickets to Stockholm—nor will they—but it does illustrate a couple of tricks you can implement in your writing to help move the story forward *and* include the appropriate balance of backstory.

1) Include backstory in scene

This couple has been married long enough to have a routine, to own a suburban home (presumably). Do we need to know how long they've been married or what prompted the desire for divorce? Maybe, but not *now*.

See? That's pacing. We release the information *slowly*, over time. We're *building*.

2) Include characterization in scene.

He drives in this relationship. His behavior is alpha; her behavior is submissive. We can tell a lot about their relationship by the limited action we've seen so far.

She wears silk to church. Do you have an idea of the kind of person who wears silk vs., say, jeans and a T-shirt? We don't need to say she's stuffy or prissy or repressed, but we can guess some of those attributes by what she's wearing.

Can we verify our suspicions? No. But that mystery *also* compels us to keep reading.

We all want to be right and your reader is no exception. She wants to Sherlock Holmes her way through your novel, and verify her suspicions along the way—which is why you should...

3) Assume your reader is smart enough to fill in the blanks.

Where does this couple live? Is it a big house or a small house? Is she a brunette or blonde?

You probably see all the details in the story you're writing. Some writers really, really, *really* want to share, like a five-year-old who can't *wait* to tell you about the frog she's caught.

Play nicely, writer friend.

Take your turn. Give your reader a chance to play too. Your reader has an imagination and wants to use it. If you give away every single detail, you're not giving your reader the chance to join in the fun.

Assume your reader is smart enough to fill in some of the blanks, and give them the opportunity to do so.

4) Start the scene *in media res.*

In media res means in the middle of the action. I didn't lead up with backstory. I just got to the heart of the matter. This won't work all the time, and it's very easy to overdo—so use it sparingly—but it can be *very* effective when done right.

(If we're making secret sauce, *in media res* is jalepeno—a little bit goes a long way.)

Nearly every action film begins *in media res,* usually with some type of action-packed chase scene. Why? It gets your attention. It's an effective hook.

5) Allow some room for your reader to ask questions.

What kind of a guy asks for a divorce after church? Was there something at church that was the final trigger? Leave some of the tension for the rest of the story. Answer your reader's questions later. That's the purpose of the rest of the chapter, and indeed the rest of the book.

6) Use symbols to create tension.

Using symbols is one of the most complicated techniques of all, and when a writer *tries* to do it, it often feels forced.

Remember when I said, "Don't call yourself a writer if you refuse to be a reader?" Here's where the reading pays off.

If you've ever tried to learn a second language, you know that reading in that second language is difficult *but* that over time, it is one of the most powerful tools for developing fluency.

Not only are you learning vocabulary, but you're learning syntax: how words go together.

When you read (in general, no need to read in a second language, but hey, whatever floats your *bateau*), you become fluent in literary devices, you no longer have to think about them or try to use them, they become part of your lexicon.

Here's what I was going for in this lil snippet:

The husband puts the car in park.
He puts a stop to things.

Lame? Too much of a stretch? Too English-y?

Consider this: I wrote the piece. I could have had him start the car. They could have been leaving for church. Consider the implications of *that* juxtaposition. He's starting something as he's asking for another thing to end? *Totally* different feeling.

I'm thinking he's having an affair.

Let's look at another:

The ice cream is melting.
Just like their relationship, it's fading away, slipping out of her fingers. It's out of her reach. She can't stop it.

At least for now. We don't know what happens when she opens the car door—for the ice cream *or* for her marriage. There's potential there, and that potential creates tension.

(So now it's a symbol *and* a tension builder. Remember the two birds thing?)

Further, the groceries indicate a future (at least of eating together) that they no longer have. The ice cream is part of those groceries, of that future, and it's melting away, slowly, in the car that's heating up under a blazing sun, a car that's stagnated in the driveway of their marriage...

Ok, that got melodramatic fast. My funny business up there ^^^ is an excellent illustration of why less is more (see clarity), why the first image did better work than the mumbo jumbo I just wrote.

A note about the process.

When I wrote the driveway passage I wasn't thinking of the elements I would use. I just set out to write a paragraph that would address tools a storyteller carries around. Once I finished, I analyzed what I had done and laid it out for you so you could do it. (Don't you hate those books where they show you awesome examples, and then give you no clue why it's so awesome or how to do it on your own?)

I'm not telling you about my process so you will send me fan mail to tell me how amazing I am; I am telling you that so you can see that you can do it too.

Years and years of reading widely have increased my knowledge base. I can draw from it, just as any reader-cum-writer can.

I wouldn't be writing this book and doing the work I do if I didn't believe that the writing process can be taught, and I don't want this moment to escape with the illusion that I am some kind of word magician. There's no magic here, only lots of years of trying and failing, and reading—and those are easily acquired if you're willing to put in the effort.

Your turn.

Give it a go. Yes, it's ok to write in your book. Ok, use a separate piece of paper if you insist.

Look at the list of elements I pulled from the air. Choose a scene from your novel and rewrite it, implementing some of these techniques.

A note on formulas

Formulas are great—if you're a *chemist*.

Have you ever read a book that had that "constructed" feel, like the same pattern over and over again?

The key for your writing is to think of Ma's sauce—there's no written recipe anywhere. She learned to make it by taste, as her ancestors did before her.

Writing is like that. You've got your end goal in mind—a completed story—but the paths that will take you there will vary.

They *should vary*—for the reader's sake, they absolutely *should* vary. No formulas allowed.

You might be tempted once you hit on something that works to keep doing that thing. Start *in media res,* use a symbol for the tension, introduce the character by comparing her to the setting...repeat.

You might think you've struck gold and want to repeat the same technique over and over again.

Do so at your own peril. You will bore the reader to tears with any kind of pattern. The thinking here isn't how easy it is to *write* your story, but the feast your readers will have when you place your well-spiced gourmet novel before them.

Remember the Weaving?

I've compared writing to a lot of things in this book, but one of the major threads is weaving or knitting. (Get it? Threads? I crack myself up. Ok, moving on.)

Why is a story called a yarn?

Well, in this day in age, few of us make clothing from yarn out of necessity (it's more of a hobby), and even fewer of us make our own yarn. Therefore, it's reasonable for most of us that the process of spinning yarn is a lost art.

Fort #4 Photograph by Annalisa Parent

It just so happens I grew up in a small town with a Colonial past and a living museum, so let me digress.

If you've ever played with yarn, you noticed it's made up a smaller threads. These are spun on a spinning wheel, or can be hand spun. To make yarn, one twirls and twirls threads (they're called plies, for the next time you're on *Jeopardy*) together until they stick together in a cohesive whole. Sounds like story-telling, right? Many threads woven together, one cohesive whole.

That's great. We've figured out how to make yarn, and weave, and knit, and we can watch countless YouTube videos if that's what we want to get into. But the pattern or recipe for writing is far less straightforward. That doesn't mean that having some kind of a visual or a map isn't helpful; it just means there isn't necessarily a one-size-fits-all.

For me as a novelist the interweaving of the plot lines is the most difficult part to conceptualize, the part where my head can spin, and I want to give up. I struggled for a long time before I came up with a system that works for me.

One of the keys to my process was figuring out that the revision is in the pacing. (See all that trouble I saved you?) By revisiting character wants and thinking about how they advanced

Secret Sauce: The revision stage is a good time to revisit character wants and think about how they support the advancement of the plot.

my plot, I was able to complete the story in a way that felt whole and complete (rather than the tangled mess I had when I completed my first draft).

I came up with a complex structure that simplifies the think-ing process for my plotting. (Ironic, ain't it?)

One of the most important pieces of work we do in the Writing Gym is to create individualized revision systems, ways to illus-trate or visualize the plot arc you've created.

Try it. How can you map out your plot so you can see the holes and make sure the structure is sound?

One of the aspects that makes revision hard is that we're jug-gling all these character arcs with plot arcs *and* trying to get the pacing down.

Make it complicated. Don't make it complicated.

One reason writing often feels difficult is conflicting advice—which is the result of the balance writing requires. When you feel overwhelmed by what feels like conflicting advice, remem-ber the cooking analogy in the mindset section. It's a standard tradition to have turkey and stuffing at Thanksgiving, right? But I bet your turkey and the neighbor's turkey look and taste and smell a little different. You still both made turkey—differ-ent recipe, different spices, different technique.

(Remember Ma's Sauce? That spaghetti photo. That was Thanksgiving; we often celebrate with a big ole platter of spa-ghetti and meatballs—but you're so smart, you probably fig-ured that out by now.)

Remember that writing is like cooking. Once you know how to make a dish, you can vary it, substitute, try different spices. But many of us the first time around with a new dish stick closely to the recipe and only vary it later.

Your mom and your grandma might tell you different ways to cook the turkey (conflicting advice) and your first time hosting Thanksgiving, you just want to get it right. When we're learning, we want to stick to the rules, and that's natural. As time goes on, you'll feel more comfortable tweaking the recipe.

When it comes to writing, follow the rules to start, but use your instincts that you get from rich reading as well. As you grow as a writer, you'll be able to improvise more, know which rules to follow and which rules to break, and when to do which.

CLARITY

ONE OF YOUR FINAL revisions will be when you go through your novel with a fine-toothed comb and think about the nuances of the reader experience. You're going to ensure that the message is as clear as can be without any extra words or confusing passages.

You've built your house, now it's time to make sure there aren't so many pillows on the sofa that your guests can't even sit down.

What does that mean? For most writers, adding more is not the issue at hand. Most writers need to take away, reduce the wordiness, give their reader some room to breathe.

Chewing GUM lose its flavor?

So many people tell me that they want to be a writer, but they're no good at grammar. Don't worry about grammar, usage and mechanics (GUM) in the first round. Is good grammar important? Of course—the clarity of your message depends on it.

Secret Sauce:
Poorly written prose gets put down, even if its message is decent.

Poorly written prose gets left behind, forgotten, abandoned—even if its message is decent.

However, grammar can always be cleaned up later. If you feel like it's not your strong suit, you can always hire a professional copy editor.

Don't overlook this step, but also do not stress about it as you are getting the story down on paper. Polish your sculpture once it's formed, but form it first.

Language is the medium through which story is delivered, like paint for painters. It's foundational. A good novel is *good*

Secret Sauce:
A good novel is good because it uses its medium—words—well; its sentences are well-crafted.

because it uses its medium well; its sentences are well-crafted.

Know any world renowned finger painters? No?

Then don't think you can get away with sloppy writing in your final draft. As we've discussed (maybe one or two times in this book), writing is a process. It's important to know *when* to focus on *what*.

Secret Sauce: Writing is a process. It's important to know *when* to focus on *what*.

Use language to your advantage, and work with a quality coaching program to help fill in your knowledge gaps.

You get what you pay for

Writers come to me all of the time with the question, "How can I find a cheap editor?"

I tell them it's very simple. Don't.

Here's the bottom line: You *must* have an editor look at your book and give you feedback. You'll want both content feedback and grammatical feedback.

No, don't tell me your beta readers did that for you. We already talked about that.

Secret Sauce: When it comes to editing, you get what you pay for. Don't Skip. Don't Skimp.

If you're serious about publishing, you need a high-quality, comprehensive, *professional* edit of your book before you submit it anywhere.

Get the best you can pay for. We'll talk more about editing later—all you need to know now is: Don't Skip. Don't Skimp.

Moving your novel from B- to A+

If you're going to go for an A game in any area as a beginning writer, I would put all of my eggs in the basket of style. One of the phrases writers hear me use often when offering feedback is, "If you want to take this novel from B- to A+, you could..." What I mean by that is that heaps of novels are published whose prose is decent, passable, acceptable—and *forgettable*.

We've talked about a lot of the greats in this book: Homer, Dostoevsky, Conrad, Hemingway, Shakespeare.

News flash: They're all dead. But we're still talking about them, enjoying their work. Why?

Because they told the most original story ever? Nope.

Because they told a relatable story *well.*

Do you want your novel to be in the 50 cent bin at someone's yard sale, or a revered possession on the shelf?

Secret Sauce:
The greats remain great because they told a relatable story *well.*

We all have an important message, a story to tell, and if you stuck with me this far, it's because you believe in telling that story in the best way of which you are capable.

So let's take a look at a few style points you can consider to augment your book.

Less is More

Remember the section on economy?

Oftentimes, using fewer words makes a better book. This concept is counterintuitive to many beginning writers

Secret Sauce:
When it comes to writing, there is more power in subtraction than addition.

who revise by adding more, more, more. (I was no exception in the beginning.) When it comes to writing, there is more power in subtraction than addition.

Cut the Melodrama

Remember what I said about equal and opposite reaction?

Secret Sauce: Don't try to be poetic when simplicity will do.

Secret Sauce: Balancing simplicity and specificity is how to move yourself on your way from B- to A+.

Well, you are going to use literary devices, but always stay away from the melodrama.

What might this look like?

Well, don't try to be poetic when simplicity will do.

Here's an example:

She looked at him and tears made their descent down her cheeks.

Why not just say "a tear ran?"

One hallmark of a beginning writer is that they often reach for a complicated word when a simple one will do.

Balancing simplicity and specificity is how to move yourself on your way from B- to A+.

When it comes to literary devices, sure, try them out, see if they ring true for your work. Just like when you were learning to talk, you'll make mistakes, but you've got to try something out first and work through the process of improving and becoming fluent.

While we've got the ax out...

While we've got the ax out and we're thinking of what we can chop, let's think about this. You're going to go through your novel and revise it several times. (Sorry. Pantser Peril.) On the first go-through you'll be cutting scenes, and on subsequent re-visions you'll cut sentences, and later still you'll go through and cut words.

How do you know what to cut? Let's take a look at the root of the problem and think about some reasons why writers might in-clude too much de-tail to begin with.

Secret Sauce: On the first go-through you'll be cutting scenes, and on subsequent revisions you'll cut sentences, and later still you'll go through and cut words.

Why is it tempting to include too much detail?

A lot of writers, especially beginning writers, fall into this trap of gratuitous detail. There was a time in literary history when lavish detail was important, and that time was in the nineteenth century.

What was happening in the olden days?

Well, there was no television, there were no movies, and there were no computers. For entertainment people sat in front of the fireplace and read aloud to each other. Because visualization took place in the imagination, including many details could be important as a means of scene-setting and providing additional entertainment.

Folks back then had a lot of long hours to sit around and read. Today, we have very fast lives; a lot to do, a lot to fit in. We don't like gratuitous detail. Literature has moved on, and we don't need to know every single aspect of that Victorian mansion— I'm sure it's beautiful, but really: three adjectives for the curtains? Move on, please.

Another interesting effect of the advent of photography, television and the Internet is a much more connected world. I say "Victorian mansion," you've got a picture in your mind. It might not be anything like the mansion in my mind, but you've got a starting point, a point of reference.

It's hard to imagine a world without photographs, but I think we can all understand that in a time before photography, the writer would have to fill in a lot of blanks for the reader.

We no longer live in that world.

Even if you're creating your own universe, you still don't need to overdo it. Want proof?

Alien Planet.

You've got a picture in your head, right? Because you've watched television and movies, read comic books, whatever. We've even got a point of reference for what we collectively imagine.

Fill in some of the blanks for your reader, but not all.

Only include details that have the sole purpose of moving the plot forward. (I feel like I'm having deja vu all over again.)

But what about grammar?

Look, look, I know. We worry more about that about which we have less confidence. It's ok if you're still stuck on grammar. So, if you *must* think about grammar, think of the words you (almost) never need.

What am I talking about here? Adverbs and present participles.

Say what?

Ok, let's review. An adverb is a word that modifies a verb...

Unscrunch your face, please.

Here's what you need to know: *Most* (not all, people, but *most*) adverbs end in -ly. Quickly, hastily, hurriedly, quaintly, quietly, loudly...you get the idea.

CUT. THEM. OUT.

You may use three *total* in your whole novel. The number shall be three and is not to exceed three.

And while I am on my adverb soapbox, there is one adverb that is very uneccessary, mostly because it is very overused, and in general, very superfluous.

Have you guessed it?

Yup, it's "very."

You may not use "very" ever.

> But what about?

No.

> But if I...?

No.

Very is very sloppy.

Nix it.

Ok, ok, ok. Stop pouting. Let me tell you what you can use: strong verbs.

He walked quickly. NO.

He dashed. YES.

He said loudly. NO.

He shouted. YES.

But where do I get all of these strong verbs?

(My, you are a persistent pouter, aren't you?)

Simple: Read.

Oh, and the other thing you can do?

Read.

Read quality writing. Read books that make you look up words.

Having a rich vocabulary means that you can write with precision; you will always choose the most accurate word (which sounds a lot like economy to me).

(To be fair, I did tell you about two hundred pages ago that writing is a vortex.)

While we are talking about fancy schmancy vocabularies, let me take a moment to address pontification.

If you utilize your expansive neoterics for the intendment of affecting sagacity, you will, forsooth, only represent grandiloquence, and your reader shall, well...do exactly what you just did.

Skip the sentence. Roll your eyes?

Yeah. Nobody likes a showoff.

Use the right word for the situation. Use the best, most specific word—which sometimes just may be the simplest word.

And before I step off my soap box (the view is quite nice from up here), let's have a little chat about the thesaurus.

Are you gratuitously thesaurusing? STOP IT. NOW. I mean it.

There's this idea in writing that you have to sound English-y, pontificating, official, in order to get your idea across. In reality, the opposite is true.

Specific words and labels help us to understand the world around us. (You need only to think of the difference between *flower* and *tulip* to know this is true.) That said, wordiness often detracts from meaning.

Many writers reach to the thesaurus to give their writing an air of authority, or to make it sound the way they think writing should sound.

Ooo, look. You've got mail—*again*.

You're quite popular, you know.

To: StubbornReader@storytellingforpantsers.com
From: *The* Stephen King
Re: Your Thesaurus

Any word you have to hunt for in a thesaurus is the wrong word. There are no exceptions to this rule.

Sincerely,
Stephen King

I call it gratuitous thesaurusing—using a thesaurus to sound official while not really enhancing or improving the meaning.

Writing is meant to communicate—whether it's a memo or a story, your point needs to come across. Writing that becomes a murky water of five-syllable words for the sake of five-syllable words is not fulfilling that purpose.

So, yes, use *tulip* instead of *flower*, if you mean *tulip*. But don't use *tulip* when *flower* would have done as well. Don't try to fluff your point to enhance your message, because it actually detracts.

Label something specifically when needed—whether it's object or action. Otherwise, try to explain your ideas in the simplest, most direct way possible. The best way to improve your writing and to get this concept down is practice, practice, practice, and (you know what I'm going to say, right?) read, read, read.

Pesky Little Present Participle

What is a present participle? Well, who cares, really? Are you going to become a grammarian?

Probably not.

Ok, ok, I will tell you, because if you're like me, you're just curious about the world. But, as I've said before, it doesn't matter if you know what any individual item in this whole universe is called if you don't know how to use it.

So, let's talk about the present continuous tense, thusly named because it describes an action that is continuing to take place in the present. I am writing. You are reading. (Did you know books are time machines?)

It's a super handy tense a lot of the time—but not so much in books.

Why? Because there are very, er, scratch that...because there are *few* cases when one is actually still doing the doing.

> He was walking across the field and he was thinking about what he would find when he got to the

other side of the stadium, to that spot behind the bleachers, where he and Jenny used to make out after practice. He was thinking and he was walking and he wasn't even chewing his gum, because he was feeling distracted.

Do you see how distracting those verbs are? Let's just get him across the field and over to Jenny, for Pete's sake!

(Who is Pete, and how did he get in my book?)

Jack walked across the field. What would he find on the other side of the stadium? What would he see, or worse *hear*, in that spot behind the bleachers where he and Jenny used to make out after practice? His gum sat unchewed in his mouth as he turned the corner and saw...

See how much cleaner that is? What did I do? Eliminated -ing.

(Well, and some other techniques too, but right now we're talking about pesky present participles.)

These little tiny tweaks can have a *big* impact on the effectiveness of your story. That's why we dedicate time every week to diving deep into these kind of details in manuscripts over in the Writing Gym. The tweaks and deletions seem so minor and nitpicky—until you read the difference.

The first book would be a chore to read, the second sounds interesting.

Same Jack. Same Jenny. Same field.

Different *words*.

We must master our medium if we are to be true artists.

Why do you have a love triangle with verb tenses?

> Jack knew he loved Jenny the moment he saw her. She has beautiful, long blonde hair that she always tied up in a bun. But it isn't just her hair. It was her smile, her laugh, the way she is kind to everyone she met. The day their trays bumped in the lunch line, Jack knew she was the one.

AGH! If that didn't hurt to read, please try again.

Look, I know it's tempting. The present tense is so cool and suave, so *now*. He just gets things done, baby. And then there's the past tense—so reliable, always there for you, rugged, solid, a rock.

Did you just get a leading role on a soap opera? Snap out of it! You *have* to choose. Your novel cannot waffle back and forth between verb tenses, no matter *what* you do in your love life.

You *have* to choose.

You cannot date the present tense and the past tense at the same time in your book.

Stop leading these poor tenses on, trailing them about.

Defecate or remove yourself from the human waste apparatus.

**Hey Smarty Pants.
Line your pockets with *this*.**

Download this free checklist to help walk you through the process of revision *and* get more bonus tips on how to bring clarity to your writing. www.writing-gym.com/revision

Over-excitement

Wow, this is so exciting! I can't believe it! This book is the best thing ever!

Are you tired yet?

Exclamation points are meant to be exciting! Another hallmark of a beginning writer is a manuscript littered with exclamation points!

Now look, my fellow writer, if you met me, you know I'm more Tigger than Eeyore. I wear my passion for life on my sleeve (must be the Italian connection, non lo so[2]), but I still don't use exclamation points in my writing.

But can I...?

Yes. Now before you get too uppity, you may have one—one exclamation mark for your *entire* book. That's a maximum. You get bonus points if you don't use any at all.

Who's driving this car?

Point of view is a sticky wicket. Writers often ask me which point of view they should use to tell their story and I can understand their confusion.

The point of view from which you tell your story dictates the flow of information you can share with your reader. Getting point of view wrong can mean difficulties with plotting and pacing.

We spend a good deal of time in the Writing Gym working through questions of point of view, batting around the merits of first person vs. third person in the context of a writer's particular work. The best strategy regarding point of view is to consider early on what and how you want to reveal so you can choose the best perspective to convey your ideas. It *is* possible to rewrite a novel to change the point of view, of course, but this is certainly a difficult task once the entire novel is written.

---

[2]   I don't know

Who you dissing?

Let's suppose you just decided your book would get published on the power of your story. Let's suppose you overlook every clarity rule I've given you because grammar's such a pain and you're not one of those English-y types, so who cares? Let's say after making this foolish assumption you ship ye ole manuscript off to an agent without considering elements of clarity.

What will happen?

Tick tock. Tick tock. (I'll give you a moment to consider your answer.)

Yes, rejection. And probably an upset stomach for the agent.

Now look, maybe you were that student who wrote your paper on the school bus the morning it was due and thought the teacher wouldn't notice. (I bet your teacher outsmarted you.)

Let's take a moment to think about agents. Why do you think they become agents?

To spy and shoot guns?

Wrong kind of agent. I mean a *literary* agent.

Right.

Because they love spending hours poring over slushy manuscripts looking for gold? Probably not. (Though I am sure most enjoy finding that one gold nugget.)

It is because they love words, literature, they love to *read*. Somewhere inside of them, that impulse (along with others, I'm sure) is at the heart of what they do.

Let's go back to the NHL analogy. If I play on a pick-up team all winter, become the best player in town, have the most goals ever on record, am I ready for NHL tryouts? No. I may be pretty good, but the people who are going to judge me are *experts*. They can spot a fake in a second. They can critique the way I hold my stick without even having to think about it. Why? It's their passion, it's their job, and it's their area of expertise.

What are you an expert in?

How does it feel when someone treats your interest like a hobby, a cute pastime? Does that make you feel good?

I'm going to imagine you said no.

If you are sending sloppy manuscripts to agents, are you treating those agents like the professionals they are? Are you showing them the respect they deserve for the positions they've earned?

No.

And they know it.

Just like your teacher did, all those years ago.

Let's just have another truthing moment, ok? It's all right if you don't want to put in the work. You don't have to. But please don't expect the agents to coo, and the readers to come flocking.

Could you be the one amazing poorly written one-hit wonder of the decade? Maybe. Why take the chance?

Style, grammar, using words effectively—these are the tools of the trade. Writers who put in the practice reap the rewards. If you're not confident in your abilities, get the support you need to take you to the next level.

HOW TO PUBLISH

So many writers dream of being published, but find themselves stuck because they can't even finish a manuscript.

That's a tragedy and just plain wrong.

Can you relate?

- Do you long to publish—but can't even finish your manuscript?
- Do you feel the same frustration I hear from so many writers who are exhausted from writing their umpteenth draft?
- Are you unsure if the feedback you're getting is trustworthy or if you really should tweak that one part?
- Have you been seeking the right class, the right book, the right conference to set you on the path to authorship and come up with nada?

Are you tired of wasting money on classes that don't help and only end up confusing you more than where you started?

And finally:

Do you wish your questions could be answered, your problems would go away, and your manuscript would just be done already?

Look, I get it. I really, really do. I've heard this story from hundreds of writers, and there was a time in my life when I was there too.

Discouraged. Afraid. Uncertain. Frustrated, and mostly confused about which direction to go and whom to trust.

We are on the *same page*. Why yes, it's page 232.

If any of those questions above resonated with you, I have good news. None of those are the real problem. Those are just the symptoms. The real problem is you've believed erroneous publishing myths.

Secret Sauce: If you're like most writers, the real publishing problem is you've believed erroneous publishing myths.

What?

Yeah.

Sorry to be the one to deliver the bad news, but there's a lot of misinformation out there.

Don't worry. It's not all bad news. You *can* break free from Pantser Peril, Lollygag Woods, Molassesn't-on-the-Chair Swamp...

Moving on.

And when you do, you'll meet and exceed your word count goals—while writing with the kind of fun that feels like summer camp. You'll feel not only supported, but confident in your writing ability and have clarity around your writing strengths.

You'll have the knowledge you need to create a publishable manuscript that's up to industry stan-

dards, but more importantly you'll know how and when that knowledge applies to your manuscript.

You'll be in a state of flow with your writing. You'll break through the struggle and live in symbiosis with your writing. You'll create it and it will feed you creatively.

You'll have a finished manuscript in which you feel confidence and pride.

I've already told you that I started out in the same writing trenches that we all do. I knew where I wanted to be; I could almost taste it. It took me years to get myself to publishable. Over time, I noticed five things successful authors were doing to get the attention of agents and publishers.

Now, I've been at this writing gig a long time. I've seen some people win and some people lose. I started to realize what the writers who publish over and over were doing to accelerate completion and publication.

So, what I'm going to do now is share what I've learned with you.

Shh! You won't tell anyone else, will you? It'll just be our little secret.

Secret Sauce:
Successful writers have their mindset in order.

(You just leaned into the book again, didn't you?)

They've got their mindset in order.

I know. I know. I know. Woo-woo again.

But, if I asked you to be *really* honest with me and rate your fear around writing: fear of messing up; fear of getting it right; fear of publishing, fear of rejection; fear of acceptance; fear of people reading your work; fear of people not liking your work...

If I asked you to rate your fear on a scale of 1 to 10:

1   *5*   *10*

|- - - - - - - - - -|- - - - - - - - - - -|

I'm Cool   *Scariest roller coaster ever meets haunted house meets Zombie Apocalypse*

What would you choose?

That number is your little secret, and you don't need to tell anyone.

What if I told you you could dial that number down several notches, master your fear, and combat it with true confidence?

Is that an elixir you'd buy?

Yeah, most writers would.

So, when I talk about mindset, it's not about getting woo-woo. It's about learning the skills to work through the fear, to move into confidence that leads to prodigious *writing*—joyous writing even.

If you don't lay this foundation, if you stay in the fear, how likely do you think you are to finish that manuscript? To send it out into the world?

Again, this is *your* number. Keep it to yourself, but be honest.

The thing is: If you're like most writers, you're not going to get anywhere close to your writing goals and dreams if you don't look at the root of the problem.

That's what so many writing classes miss—classes teach how to sketch a character without taking into account the writer as a person, without taking a holistic view of the writer—his talents, his needs, his fears—and so year after year, class after class churns out writer after writer—and none of them gets published.

Because they didn't have enough knowledge, or best-selling authors as professors?

No.

Because no one showed them how to work through their fear, which *must* be the foundation of a quality writing program, or writers will continue to flop and fail.

Writers who get mindset right not only write more—more words and more often—they do so with more joy. Writing becomes fun again. It's something they always have time for because it's enjoyable.

If you feel stuck, like you don't have time to write, the real culprit is not knowing how to deal with your fear, and I'm here to tell you that a quality program will give you the skills to work through that.

Let's do the timewarp (again)

Let us describe a classroom, shall we?

Your typical classroom has desks or tables where students sit. Where is the teacher in your vision?

At the front of the classroom.

Doing what?

Talking.

What are the students doing?

Listening.

Here's the bottom line: Despite over a century of pedagogical and neuroscientific research demonstrating the futility of this type of instruction, most classes—whether elementary school, high school or college—are still run this way.

Writing classes are no exception.

Most writing classes are a teacher telling you *what* something is or, if you're lucky, *how* to do something, but without giving you repeated feedback on your progress.

This is why it's time to ditch class.

It's not you. Really.

So many writers come to me thinking something is wrong with them because they just don't get it—why haven't they figured out this writing thing yet? They've taken so many classes—what gives?

Let's take a stroll down memory lane to your high school years.

(No need to tell anyone what year that is; that's another safe little secret.)

Now, I want you to think of a teacher you hated (no, you have to pick *one*, you can't say all of them).

I want you to choose a teacher whose class was *BO-RING*, a place where you felt like you learned virtually nothing.

Let's just call that teacher Smith.

Now I want you to think of an awesome teacher, one who taught something you thought was pretty boring, but there was just something about that teacher that made the subject fun, exciting, and even (gulp) something to look forward to.

Let's call that teacher Jones.

What did Jones know that Smith didn't? What did Jones do that Smith didn't?

Whatever you say, I bet it's going to fall under the umbrella of engagement. He made you laugh. She planned fun activities. The classroom was hands-on.

What was the focus? YOU.

The learner. The student experience.

Let me tell you a secret about your lil ole noggin: It learns best by doing, getting feedback, and trying again.

Secret Sauce:
Your brain learns by doing, getting feedback, and trying again.

But what do writing classes do? You sit, you listen, you take notes.

Maybe you write to a prompt and share what you wrote. Maybe you hand in some pages and get a little feedback. Those are steps in the right direction, but they're a far cry from the ongoing feedback loop that leads to real progress and confidence in a skill.

These classes give you lots of information, but very little experience trying it, getting feedback, and trying it again. Do you need knowledge? Of course. But writing is a craft, and as such, takes time and experience to become proficient.

While we're walking down memory lane, let's journey back in human history to the Middle Ages.

Way back in medieval times, people who made stuff (bakers, tanners, shoemakers, etc.) didn't go to Stuffmaking University; they trained under a Master Craftsman. They started in their youth, and trained for five to nine years to learn the craft. After that, they *still* weren't considered Masters, but had to prove their salt as a Journeyman.

What's my point? (Well, that I have a slight obsession with medieval history, but beyond that...)

Craft takes time to learn, and it's not learned sitting in hallowed ivy-covered halls. Just like the apprentices of the Middle Ages, we learn by doing, by getting feedback from a Master, from trying again, by watching, by immersing ourselves in the learning experience.

Is your writing class doing that for you?

I'm going to guess no, as that was one of the major frustrations I had as a beginning writer and which I still hear writers talk about today. No individualization. Cursory feedback. Not enough time dedicated to making attempts and getting feedback.

This style of writing class is a dime a dozen out there in the writing world. Sage on the Stage, teacher-centered and, for the most part, useless, or worse: doing more harm than good.

What do I mean?

These types of classes help a writer to procrastinate because he gets overwhelmed with information or finds out so many more rules and tricks and grammar that he thinks he needs to know about, so he spends his time confused or down the rabbit hole of fruitless Google searches.

Here's a hard truth: These institutions of "learning" want you to stay stuck in this loop because if you continue to be confused, you'll continue to give them money to be unconfused.

If you actually figure out how to write and publish a novel, you'll no longer be of use to them.

These types of institutions have put you in intentional discomfort to continue to milk money from you a little at a time, year after year.

What would you say of a parent who didn't teach their kid to walk, for fear that once the child could, he would leave? Good parenting? No. Self-serving. We'd call that abuse.

A quality writing program has the goal of you completing your manuscript, publishing, and moving out of the nest. Fly, little bird, and soar. Invite me to your book launch.

That's a good program.

Hey Smarty Pants.
Line your pockets with *this*.

If you're looking for that kind of progress in your writing and the attributes of the kind of program that can take you there, you can download my free checklist *Ditch the Writing Class: Attributes of a Quality Writing Program* here. There's even a free video to help walk you through the steps to find quality programs. www.writing-gym.com/publish

You don't need a class. You need a program.

If you want to publish a book, you're shooting for the Stanley Cup (remember the hockey analogy?) and you need the kind of systematic support that will help you to get there.

Depending on your source, something between 80 to 90% of the population wants to write a book. Do you know how many millions of people that is? That's, like, a lot.

Secret Sauce: You don't need a class. You need a writing program.

But how many people *actually* do it—finish writing the book and get it published?

According to the Bowker Report, we churn out about 300,000 traditionally published books per year in the US. Now, you don't have to be a statistician to see that—even though 300k is a lot of books—that's still just a small proportion of the people who want to write books getting published every year.

What about self-publishing? Well, according to the same report, 700,000 books were self-published in 2015. That shows that 700,000 people finished a book. Not too shabby...well, until you consider the 20 million or so who said they had a book in them.

What happened to the other 19,000,000 people?

Why didn't they finish a book to publishable?

Let's take a look around your writing room, shall we? Oh look, a book shelf. (Don't be embarrassed about the dust—no one dusts anymore.)

Ooo, look at all these books on writing, and magazines, and course materials, and workbooks, ticket stubs from writing conferences. You've been busy.

Are you not published yet because you don't have the right information? You've got loads of information here: plot, character, point of view, how to find an agent, query letters, elevator pitch...it's all here.

Is the lack of information holding you back?

No.

So, what's the *real* culprit?

You need the application of all that knowledge to *your* specific manuscript and the accountability to get the writing done. *That* is what differentiates a writing *program* from a writing *class*.

My question for you is: Do you need more writing instruction? Or do you need to know how to apply all of those concepts to your writing: how to apply that information about plot to *your* story? How to apply those principles of character to *your* protagonist?

Do you need to find the time to write and find the support you need to get there? Or do you need one more class on plot structure?

The tragedy here for people who just accumulate and accumulate knowledge year after year without ever really learning to apply it, is they end up a statistic. Yup, they're part of the 19 million people who had a passion, had a book in them, and... nothing.

That makes me sad just thinking about it.

An unrealized dream.

There are probably sadder tragedies in the world, but I view unrealized dreams as one of the saddest things going. Unrealized potential. The loss of letting go of something you never even got to hold in your hands? Heartbreaking.

I'm picturing this person walking down the sidewalk on one of those wintery windy days where you tuck your chin into your collar. Everything is that dirty gray of winter. The wind whips up and blows his scarf, so he looks up at the advertisement pasted to the wall beside him, larger than life, a new book by a bestselling author. *How many books does that guy get to publish anyway? And I can't even finish one. His books aren't even really that good. I know I could write something better, if I could just...*

Winter just got a whole lot bleaker.

Are you rooting for this guy? Let's call him Tom. Do you want Tom to see that there's another way? If he would just shift his focus from a class to a program...

Tom, Tom, can you hear me? There's a better way.

Did you just talk to a book?

What if it worked, your talking to the book? Let's play this out. What if your message reached Tom and he changed his ways, signed up for a program that gave him the support he needed, and showed him how to apply the principles of quality craft to his story?

Maybe Tom would say something like what a writer told me recently while we were working together. "Talking to you really forces me to dig deep, and really helps me to find the purpose of what I am writing, and why I am writing it."

Purpose? Do you want Tom to find purpose?

Do you want his bleak winter to be over; for the sun to shine upon his writing, his book, his *life?*

Ok, ok, ok, a little too much Eeyore there. Let's rein it back in.

But let's think about it seriously for a moment. When we are in our purpose, when we feel that sense of flow with our work—I think that's one of the best feelings in the world.

I'd want that for Tom. In the same way that I want that for you.

The writer I was working with went on to say, in that moment, that our work together helped her to know what to leave out of her novel.

Sometimes people say small ideas that lead to deep thought. Does that happen to you?

For me, this offhand comment made me start to think about all the advice out there, kill your darlings and whatnot. *How? Which ones? When? What are my darlings?* These are legitimate questions writers ask and we problem solve every day. It had become such an ingrained part of the work we do, I'd forgotten, on that day, how important having a guiding hand can be in the writing process. I thanked that writer for the important reminder of how powerful the work we do can be.

Moving from a class model into a comprehensive program can be a transformative experience. I've seen it time and time again, but no matter how many times I see a writer finish a manuscript in a place of joy and confidence, I am grateful and inspired.

These writers had the synthesis they needed to connect concepts to their application. As if that's not powerful enough, they also had the accountability to keep them writing, to meet their own expectations.

I can't even believe that no one else has caught on to the importance of accountability in a quality writing program.

Let's be honest. (*Really* honest.) If you didn't have boss who could walk in at any moment, would you be as productive? Most people would say, "Probably not." Accountability keeps us from goofing off when we should be working.

The same is true for writing. Having someone to keep you accountable is an amazing tool. It leads to real productivity too, because of the individualized attention that a quality program offers.

Without the accountability and support to meet goals, writers flail. They'll "get to it" (but they never do). They waste time *thinking* about writing without getting any typing done.

(Raise your hand if you've done that one.)

What if my character did...? How was my character born? I wonder if my character is allergic to peanut butter.

Secret Sauce: Without the accountability and support to meet goals, writers flail.

Lots of thinking, not a whole lot of writing.

In my beginning years, I had a note on my writing desk that said, "If you want to be a writer, write."

Simple as that. What do writers do? Write.

Do they brainstorm, file, read email, surf Facebook, organize all the sticky notes in rainbow order in the drawer?

Yes, they do those things...but they're not part of the job description. *Writing* is.

Secret Sauce:
If you're not writing, you're not finishing. And if you're not finishing, you're not publishing.

If you're not writing, you're not finishing. And if you're not finishing, you're not publishing.

I know we all like a good diagram. Let's take a looky here:

Accountability ↪ *Writing* ↪ *Finishing a manuscript* ↪ *Publishing*

Now look, not every manuscript gets published, of course. But I don't know a single agent who wants to represent your novel based on a half-written concept. You want to publish? You need a finished novel.

You want a finished novel? Accountability.

(We're not building Sputnik, people. Pretty easy stuff, really.)

Easy—yet so many classes don't offer accountability or the kind of support that leads to writing, and the writers in these classes wait until the last minute to hand in the chapter that's due—because it's due, which is like accountability without any meaningful support—but the writing's not done *well*, because there were dishes to do, and dogs to walk, and the writing got put off till 10 PM the night before.

Does that sound like a quality writing experience to you?

Sounds stressful.

And we all remember what happens to creativity in the brain when stress is hanging around.

Good ideas? Bye-bye.

Inspiration? Bye-bye.

Your brain's in lockdown.

Hello, Writer's Block.

No wonder so many writers give up finishing a manuscript. That sounds awful!

You couldn't *pay* me to sign up for that torture, nevermind pay *for* it.

That's crazy talk.

I know that writing can be joyful, *fun*, inspiring—one of the Writing Gym writers recently said, "It's like going to summer camp."

Think about that. Back in the day, full fun days, getting up early, staying up late, and loving every minute. Imagine having that kind of joy and enthusiasm in your writing. If writing felt like summer camp, I'd be pretty psyched. I mean, that's something you would jump out of bed in the morning for, right?

That's why these writers meet and exceed their goals every single week. Because it's *fun*. Because writing becomes something they look forward to. Because writing is something they've fallen in love with again.

What would that feel like for you?

That kind of joy, that fun, that getting back into the flow of inspiration. That's why I recommend and run a program instead of a class. Writers need a *system* not just a Sage on the Stage class.

Let's review, shall we?

Old Way	*New Way*
Sage on Stage	Participation
Information Based	Integration of Knowledge and Skills
Class	Program
Drudgery & Stress	Joy & Fun

This new approach is better than anything else out there because it is holistic. It treats the writer like the complex person she is. It recognizes that writing isn't just about knowing the right stuff. It's about doing the hands-on work, and getting quality feedback on progress. It's about knowing how to apply concepts to actual manuscripts, making the time to write again, and doing it joyfully. And, most importantly, it sits on a foundation that nurtures writers from fear to functioning, and from functioning to fun.

While we're thinking about the mind, let's talk about your brain again.

Getting the Feedback loop right

What most writing groups are doing is all wrong.

Why wrong? You ask.

Remember the brain?

Secret Sauce: Successful writers get the feedback loop right.

The majority of groups out there overlook the stages of the writing process, and they overlook the way the brain was meant to function.

Think back to the writing group we talked about before. The one where the writer writes a piece, hands it out, reads it aloud, and then everyone offers feedback.

They ask questions, and offer direction, and give critique on the reliability of the narrator, and say, "It would be better if..."

I bet you've walked out of that kind of writing group frustrated, or at the very least flabbergasted.

Why?

This is what it looks like when writing groups mix up the two phases of the writing process, and when that happens, it's like wires crossing in your brain.

The different phases of the writing process come from different centers in your brain. It's like putting on hockey gear, showing up for practice, and suddenly it's basketball season, so you change into your basketball clothes and return—only to find everyone ice skating.

Your brain doesn't know what to do.

Earlier we talked about the parts of the brain: reptilian brain, limbic system, and neocortex; and how they serve different functions. Remember emotional hijacking and how one part of the brain effectively shut down another?

Secret Sauce: Emotional hijacking is a regular occurrence in the bulk of writing groups.

Well, emotional hijacking is a regular occurrence in the bulk of writing groups.

One of the main problems is that most writers, writing groups, and instructors don't even know about the two different phases of the writing process because they don't understand how the brain works.

So, we keep on with this wrong kind of feedback—and institutions blaming writers for not being motivated enough—or wanting it enough—when they don't finish a manuscript, when the very class these writers have been reaching out to for support is working against them.

Sound warped to you?

Yeah.

Writers in these classes are like the backwards marathon runners I mentioned. They're trying their best to move toward the finish line, their coaches are on the sidelines shouting out techniques to use—but all the while they're using the machine wrong.

(There's a reason we run marathons facing forward, after all.)

Now look, the coaches mean well. They don't know any better. They don't know that they're working against the writer's brain, or that their coaching is doing more harm than good.

But that doesn't mean their techniques aren't harmful.

Remember when we talked about #FeedbackHorrorStory? That's what I'm talking about here. You've got one. I know you do. (Have you tweeted it to me yet?) Anger. Discouragement. Bullying. These are the stories I hear on a regular basis.

Secret Sauce:
Ditch the free writing group. They're not free. They're costing you a lot.

This is why one of my first pieces of advice to writers is to *ditch* the free writing group. They're not free. They're costing you a lot.

The lack of expertise, not just on writing, but on *how* to give *quality* feedback, is harming your writing and your writing future.

Sounds pretty dang expensive to me.

There's got to be a better way.

And there is.

A system—a *program*—based on how your brain actually works.

Writers in brain-based systems experience feedback that is custom-tailored. No cookie cutter or vague comments, but specific feedback that addresses craft as it applies to the writer's manuscript. That kind of feedback helps you to become a better, more confident writer. That kind of feedback makes writers say, "I grow as a writer every time."

Do you feel like you grow from the feedback you're getting now? Most writers would say no. They'd say they feel deflated after a group session, or at the very least they got decent feedback on a writing piece. But growth as a writer? Rarely.

Classes not based on the way your brain works will leave you dangling in the wind every single time.

Programs based on neuroscience will make you say, as one recent writer did, "The session gave me a confidence boost." Or another who said, "I came out with way more confidence in my writing."

How would you like to go from feeling like a deflated, soggy, used balloon to a high-flying helium balloon after a session instead?

Sign me up, right?

This method works. Writers have walked away from one session and written for an entire weekend, to come up with a finished product that was published. Seriously, want to talk about secret sauce? This is it, baby.

When your feedback is based on the way your brain actually works, you can soar forward, do things you only imagined possible, write like you always wanted to write in full confidence and flow.

Invest in a Program that Works

Let's say that you want to learn how to ride a bike.

So you take a free class that shows you how to move the pedals around and around, and you study diagrams on how the chain makes the wheels move. It's a free class, but there's not much information offered. You're not ready to ride a bike yet.

So you sign up for the $100 class at the rec center. Because it's offered by the municipality, they're safety conscious, so they teach you about the importance of wearing a helmet and the consequences of not using hand signals, and the rules for bike lanes and walking your bike on the sidewalk.

Do you know how to ride a bike yet? Nope. You haven't even sat on one.

Ok, fine. You sign up for the $500 class at the local bike shop. It's pretty cool because it includes a little pamphlet that explains the physics of how a bike balances and momentum and such.

The instructor gets on the bike and rides around the parking lot.

Don't do that. *Do* do that. Hold this here. Put your foot here. Ok, go home and practice.

Crash landing.

Next day, he shows you again how to ride a bike and he has you stand next to your bike and demonstrates where to place your hands on the handlebars.

Great. Go home and practice.

After a full week of demonstrations and small exercises, you still can't ride a bike, so you spend $1,000 on the next level class.

On and on this goes.

When we read a silly story about a would-be bicycle rider, the absurdity is clear. Yet most of the aspiring authors I meet treat their writing futures this way, every single day for year after year after year.

Spending their money in small increments and getting little to no results.

What's wrong with this approach?

Well, instead of asking, "What's the cost?" writers should be asking, "What's the value?"

Secret Sauce: Successful writers invest in a writing program that works.

What's the value in a $500 course that shows you how to do something, but doesn't give you the opportunity to try it and get feedback? Not much.

What's the real cost? Wasting valuable time instead of being in a program where you could actually be achieving what you set out to do.

Take a moment to think about that. When it comes to your writing, have you been focusing on value? Or have you been overlooking the *true* cost of hodge podging all of these writing classes and workshops and free pamphlets together?

I was talking with one of our writers and we were joking around about how much he'd wasted on writing classes before he joined our program and it was $10,000 or something close to that—just under, just over. No matter what the number, that's way too much to be wasting—without any results.

Even with all those classes, all that information, he hadn't been able to *finish* a novel nevermind publish one.

What's at stake if you continue this kind of approach?

Many years wasted trying to patchwork together a writer's life when you could have been writing and publishing, getting the results you want.

Years of wondering why you're not good enough when you could have been accessing a system that actually optimized your brain and made you more confident.

When we focus on cost, we see everything that's in the way. When we focus on value, we start to see how we can grow. We focus on goals and outcomes and where we want to go; we start to see the possibility in ourselves and how we can get there.

Do you want to be a writer, or do you want to be a perpetual class taker?

Look, there's nothing wrong with lifelong learning. I'm a big fan; continued education is central to my life's philosophy.

But there's a big difference between taking class after class after class and never learning how to ride a bike and becoming a proficient road biker and branching out to learn mountain biking or how to pop a wheelie.

The first biker is stagnated and the second biker is growing.

So, when it comes to your writing life—which one do you want to be?

You can either take the information I've given you in this book and forget all about it, keep struggling to finish your book and to get published. Or, if you want to accelerate your writing, finish your novel to publishable, and gain the kind of confidence that gets you over your fears, here's what you can do.

Whatever the biggest challenges are for you right now, my team and I, we've seen it and we know how to fix it. I love to talk to writers about where they are, where they want to be, and how they can get there. I've made space in my calendar every week just to talk to the people who had the patience to make it all the way to the end of my book. We can get on the phone or a Skype call for about 45 minutes to an hour, and on this session I will work with you to create a step-by-step game plan to move you toward your writing goals.

When we chat, we're going to get you clear on the best course of action for your writing *now*.

Let's get back to the truth, though: this isn't for everyone. If you're not looking to complete a manuscript in the next couple of months, if you're not serious about creating the very best manuscript that you can, if you're not ambitious to publish in the most prominent way possible, then now is not the right time for you.

I offer this opportunity at no cost, so of course, some people ask me why I do it. Here's why: As I was coming up in the writing world, many people reached out their hand and helped me. (I've written about many of them in this book.) I love giving back to writers who are in the same position that I was then.

Also, I know that you might want my help to transform your writing and your writing life. (And besides, after reading this book, you know just how cool I am to hang out with, right?)

If it looks like a good fit for us to work together, we can chat about that on the call. If not, that's fine too. No matter what, you'll get tremendous value from the conversation.

Here's the link to drop yourself right into my calendar that's just for the readers of this book.

www.datewiththemuse.com/pantsers

When you go there, you'll see all the available appointment times. Just grab whichever one works for you, and there will be a short application so I can get to know you a little bit. After that we'll get on the call (or on Skype) and it's going to be the best hour you've ever spent working on your book.

Thank you for sticking with me all the way to the end of *Storytelling for Pantsers* and indulging my wonky sense of humor and love of obscure cultural references. I sincerely hope this book has helped you to become a better writer and to reach out for the kind of support that helps you to become a published author.

I've put together a list of the free resources offered in the book. You can find that over in the appendix, so don't forget to take advantage of those.

Keep in touch. Keep me posted on your progress.

Annalisa Parent
Longmont Colorado
June 2017

Hey Smarty Pants.
Line your pockets with *this*.

Want a comprehensive list of all the handouts from this book? Get the Handout Handout here www.writing-gym.com/handouts

RESOURCES

A complete, one-stop-shop guide to all this book's free handouts. Get your own copy at www.writing-gym.com/handouts

Pantsing
>**Title:** A Note-Taking Outline (For People Who Don't Outline)
>**Benefits:** You know you want to take notes. Well, we've got you covered. Download the free *Storytelling for Pantsers* notetaking outline.
>**URL:** www.writing-gym.com/notes

Optimizing Your Brain's Innate Power
>**Title:** Neuroscientific Writing Prompts
>**Benefits:** Want some great writing prompts based on neuroscience and guaranteed to jump you into writing flow? Watch the video series.
>**URL:** www.writing-gym.com/brain

Finding the Confidence to Write
Title: Writing Gym Accountability Calendar
Benefits: This accountability calendar will keep you on track with your writing goals. We use this tool in the Writing Gym as part of our accountability sessions and have great results. BONUS: Tips on battling procrastination!
URL: www.writing-gym.com/accountability

Reading
Title: Annalisa's Reading List for Successful Writing
Benefits: Curious what books are on my nightstand? Download my top ten book list. **URL:** www.writing-gym.com/readbooks

How to Find the Kind of Support You Need to Help you Be Your Very Best Writer
Title: Are you getting the support you need?
Benefits: Download this simplified flowchart to walk you through the steps to find quality support to help move you toward your writing goals.
URL: www.writing-gym.com/support

Character
Title: Recipe for Successful Characters
Benefits: Get to know your characters with this non-traditional character questionnaire.
URL: www.writing-gym.com/characters

Character
Title: Discovering a system to make the pantsing process work
Benefits: Know the right questions to ask yourself so that pantsing works for you and your book.
URL: www.writing-gym.com/pantsing

Plot
Title: Plot Cards for Pantsers
Benefits: Keep track of your plot with these Writing Gym plot cards.
URL: www.writing-gym.com/plotcards

Balance
Title: Balancing your book: A Video
Benefits: Hear more writing earworms in this video *From Mire to Page-Turning Momentum: Three Plotting Mistakes that Keep Writers in the Slush Pile.*
URL: www.writing-gym.com/balance

Economy
Title: Keeping up the Pace: Moving your Plot Forward
Benefits: This table will help you verify that all of your plot points are serving to move your plot forward.
URL: www.writing-gym.com/economy

Clarity
Title: Revision Checklist
Benefits: When it comes to revision, there's a lot to think about. Download this free checklist to help walk you through the process *and* get more bonus tips on how to bring clarity to your writing.
URL: www.writing-gym.com/revision

How to Publish
Title: Ditch the Writing Class: Attributes of a Writing Program
Benefits: Ensure that your Writing Program is serving you with this handy video and checklist.
URL: www.writing-gym.com/publish

Resources
Title: The Handout Handout
Benefits: A complete, one-stop-shop guide to this book's free handouts.
URL: www.writing-gym.com/handouts

Also available as a workbook. See
www.writing-gym.com/handouts
for more information.

WORKS CITED

Alvarez, Julia. *In the Time of Butterflies.* Chapel Hill, NC: Algonquin Books of Chapel Hill, 2010.

Baldwin, Harper Lee. *To Kill a Mockingbird.* New York, NY: Grand Central Publishing, 1988.

Brixey, Andi and Annalisa Parent. *How to Find the Story and Tell it With Best Seller John David Mann*, podcast audio, The Writing Gym Podcast, MP3, accessed May 24 2017, https://writing-gym.com/bestseller/

Brixey, Andi and Annalisa Parent. *How to Get Your Nonfiction Book Published with a Major Publisher with Jill Schiefelbein*, podcast audio, The Writing Gym Podcast, MP3, accessed May 24 2017, https://writing-gym.com/majorpublisher/

Brixey, Andi and Annalisa Parent. *How to Sell Your Book with the Go-Giver's Bob Burg*, podcast audio, The Writing Gym Podcast, MP3, accessed May 24 2017, https://writing-gym.com/gogiver/

Burg, Bob, and John David Mann. *The Go-Giver, Expanded Edition: A Little Story About a Powerful Business Idea.* New York, NY: Penguin Random House, 2015.

Collins, Suzanne. *The Hunger Games.* New York, NY: Scholastic Books, 2008.

—. *Catching Fire.* New York, NY: Scholastic. 2009.

—. *Mockingjay.* New York, NY: Scholastic. 2010.

Conrad, Joseph. *Heart of Darkness.* New York, NY: Alfred A. Knopf, 1993.

Dickens, Charles. *A Tale of Two Cities.* New York, NY: Black & White Classics, 2014.

Dostoevsky, Fyodor. *Crime and Punishment.* Translated by Constance Garnett. New York, NY: Barnes & Noble Books, 2015.

Ehard, Michelle, ed. *The Portable MFA in Creative Writing.* New York, NY: Writer's Digest, 2006.

Fielding, Helen. *Bridget Jones's Diary: A Novel.* New York, NY: Penguin Books, 1999.

Frozen. Directed by Chris Buck and Jennifer Lee. USA: Walt Disney Pictures, 2013. Blu Ray.

Goleman, Daniel. *Emotional Intelligence: Why It Can Matter More than IQ.* New York, NY: Bantam Books, 1995.

Hamlet. Directed by Gregory Doran. BBC, 2009, DVD.

Harry Belafonte, "(There's a) Hole in the Bucket," in *The Essential Harry Belafonte,* Sony Music Studios, 2005, https://open.spotify.com/track/4UW7lN6GdkpN6hwxcP1DlH.

The Holy Bible, New International Version. Grand Rapids: Zondervan Publishing House, 1984.

Homer. *The Odyssey.* Translated by Robert Fagles. New York, NY: Penguin Books, 1997.

Hugo, Victor. *Les Miserables.* New York, NY: Signet Classics, 2013.

James, Henry. "The Art of Fiction." In *Literary Criticism: Essays on Literature, American Writers, English Writers*. Edited by Leon Edel and Mark Wilson. Library of America., 1984. 45-64.

Johnson, Spencer. *Who Moved My Cheese?: An Amazing Way to Deal with Change in Your Work and in Your Life*. New York, NY: G.P. Putnam Sons Publishers, 2002.

Kidd, Sue Monk. *The Secret Life of Bees* New York, NY: Penguin Books, 2003.

King, Stephen. *On Writing: 10th Anniversary Edition: A Memoir of the Craft*. New York, NY: Pocket Books, 2010.

Mays, Kelly J., ed. *The Norton Introduction to Literature*. 11 ed. New York, NY: W.W. Norton & Company, 2013.

Milne, A.A.. *Winnie the Pooh*. New York: Dutton Children's Books. 1988.

Paine, Thomas. *The Crisis*. Philadelphia: 1776

Ray, Robert J., and Bret Norris. *The Weekend Novelist*. New York, NY: Billard Books, 2005.

Rowling, J.K. *Harry Potter and the Chamber of Secrets*. New York, NY: Arthur A. Levine Books, 1999.

Shakespeare, William. *The Winter's Tale*. New York, NY: Washington Square Press, 2005.

Shakespeare, William. *Hamlet*. New York, NY: Washington Square Press, 2005.

Suess, Dr. *Oh, the Places You'll Go!* New York, NY: Random House Children's Books, 1960.

Tom and Jerry. Directed by William Hanna, Joseph Barbera, Gene Deitch, Chuck Jones, Maurice Noble, Abe Levitow, Tom Ray and Ben Washam. Written by William Hanna, Joseph Barbera, Gene Deitch, Eli Bauer, Larz Bourne, Michael Maltese, Jim Pabian, Bob Ogle, John W. Dunn. Cartoon Network.

Watterson, Bill. *Calvin and Hobbes*. Kansas City, MO: Universal Press Syndicate, 1987.

Williams, Margery. *The Velveteen Rabbit*. New York, NY: Delacorte Press, 1958.

FINAL COMMENTS

What the writing process for *Storytelling for Pantsers* looked like:

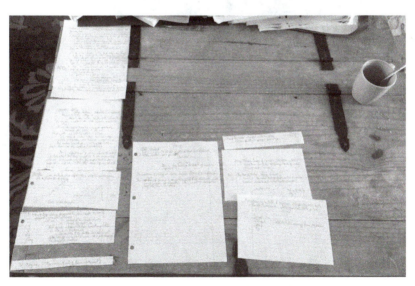

Here are my notes for the chapter on pacing. Before I make an outline, I arrange my notes in the order I want to place them in the book. This process helps me to achieve clarity before I start writing.

Except sometimes. Here is the "How to Publish" chapter, outline attempt #3. Sometimes I have to take what I've written, reread, and reorder to get my bearings. I like the tactile experience of moving bits of paper about.

The answer to riddle on page 154 is "The Winter's Tale"

ACKNOWLEDGEMENTS

It's so cliché, but until you're the one writing these words, you don't know how true they are.

This book was a team effort in so many ways. Yes, my name appears on the cover, but this book would not have been possible without the help of these truly *amazing* people:

Jill Schiefelbein and Bob Burg: for being all around cool and for letting me include their words in my book.

John David Mann: for his positive energy, encouragement, and friendship—and for saying awesome things about my book.

Faithe Thomas, my publisher, Ingrid Hedbor, my editor, and Sharon Castlen, my publicist.

You pushed, you prodded. We laughed. We cried. I couldn't have done it without you. And, Ingrid, thanks thanks for reading my manuscript so many times it appeared in your dreams.

Beth Brodovsky, your graphic advice was invaluable. Tony Galle—what amazing artwork. Thank you. Jeff Wainer, you are a patient man and a talented artist. Thank you for executing such powerful graphics from my despicable pencil sketches.

Andi Brixey, none of this—not one single moment—would have been possible without you by my side. Thank you for your encouragement, for letting me rant, for ranting with me, and for being the best right hand gal I could ever ask for.

Myles Day, your positivity and work ethic inspire me daily. Thank you for the passion and gusto you brought to this project to help make it the cohesive whole it is today.

Hannah Green, without you there would be no book. You are patient and thorough. Your hard work will be forever interwoven into every page of this book. *Thank you* for your detailed work and for keeping my head on (mostly) straight through the writing process.

And especially to all of the writers in the Writing Gym who have trusted me to be a part of your writing and publishing journey. I am blessed, honored, and eternally grateful.

Love the Secret Sauce

Visit www.storytellingforpantsers.com to get your
Secret Sauce Desk Reminder Kit today.

Secret Sauce:
Quality feedback is vital to a
publishable manuscript.

About the Author

ANNALISA IS THE SENIOR editor of Laurel Elite Books and a 2002 and 2015 Vermont Teacher of the Year nominee for her use of neuroscientific principles. She applies these same principles to her work with writers to create confidence and success.

She writes for many local, national, and international publications, has written and produced sketches for a Telly-Award winning television show. She is a firm believer in the Oxford Comma, but will defer to the Official style guidelines when necessary, or when her editor insists.

You can find out more about Annalisa and her work with writers at www.writing-gym.com.

An enthusiastic extrovert, she always loves to hear from writers. Drop her a line on twitter @annalisaparent

9 781947 482012